Trial & Error

Bronnie Quinn

Cushing Publishing
www.cushingpublishing.com

Copyright 2024 Bronnie Quinn
ISBN: 978-1-963661-16-3

Cushing Publishing
9380 Driver Road
Middlesex, NC 27557

I dedicate this book to my beloved wife, Sherry, and my two sons, Travis and Bret. Their unwavering support and involvement in this project, from Sherry's assistance in typing to Travis and Bret's help in choosing the right words, have been invaluable. This book is as much theirs as it is mine.

Acknowledgments

I also wish to acknowledge two friends who supported me in completing this work. Jim Winters repeatedly told me I should write my stories, and Matthew Brinkley wanted to know it was done. I had much encouragement to finish this book, none more than these two who wished it ended. They wanted my stories to be told by me, not someone else, for generations. Of course, without their encouragement, it would never have happened.

This book is a tribute to my late friend, Larry Jones, whose influence on my career in the highway patrol and private investigation business was profound. His insightful advice, particularly when I struggled to think independently, shaped my understanding of efficient business management. Without his guidance, my journey may have taken a different course. Larry's role in my life is a testament to the power of mentorship in shaping one's journey, and his memory will always be cherished.

This dedication is rooted in the first verse of the fifty-first chapter of the Old Testament of Isaiah:

"Look to the rock from which you were hewn,

And to the hole of the pit whence ye were dug."

Prologue

I've had so many beautiful experiences in law enforcement. I had a terrific time in the Police Department, the Sheriff's Department, and the North Carolina State Highway Patrol. Early in my career, I read a book by Dr. Albert Coats that summarized the history of the Highway Patrol. Dr. Coats stated that the State Highway Patrol was organized on July 1, 1929. The twenty-seven men with the highest grades in the first basic Patrol School were sworn into the original membership of the State Highway Patrol and named "Trooper." Those men were sworn into office by the State Highway Commissioner: "On your shoulders rests the responsibility of the success or failure of the State Highway Patrol.

Upon reading these words, I solemnly vowed that I would never be the reason the highway patrol did not endure. This commitment, this unwavering dedication to the cause, has been a guiding force in my career.

I have made mistakes during my career—probably no more than any other officer, but still more than I would sometimes like to admit. Many of the officers you will hear about in my stories, and I have always tried our best to support each other and lift the people around us.

People make mistakes, but I never wanted *my* mistakes to be why others would not succeed. I worked to make sure of that. The job of being a trooper has always been arduous. Imagine the weight of every choice those first twenty-seven men made. By the end of the second day after the State Highway Commissioner gave those men their charge, there would only be twenty-six troopers for the entire state. Trooper George Ira Thompson would give his life when an underage driver hit his motorcycle. Trooper Thompson was introducing the new troopers to the citizens of North Carolina. Originally, motorcycles were given to Troopers,

6

whereas supervisors or "officers" were given cars.

My job in 1978 was to make weekly reports, but the troopers in 1929 had to make daily reports to their supervisor, who would compile them all and send them to the commander.

Despite having to ride a motorcycle, sometimes in freezing weather, the officers did not have adequate uniforms for the weather. There are stories of troopers getting home with frozen uniforms and having to stand them up to thaw out.

Dr. Coats's book quotes one directive as follows:

"Since the primary function of the patrol is 'road patrol,' inclement weather is not an excuse for failure to comply with regulations. It is not necessary to ride motor equipment any great distance in inclement weather; bad hills, curves, and approaches to grade crossings and bridges should be guarded, and motorists should be warned of any danger lurking ahead. There is only one interpretation of this rule, and failure to comply will result in disciplinary action."

Another area for improvement with the new job of the highway patrol was the respect and approval of county sheriffs and city police. They earned that respect by working together and helping local officers in local law enforcement. They earned it at football games, other sports events, and county and state fairs. They earned it at fires and floods. They earned it at celebrations of historical events. They earned respect by handling law and labor disputes and other confrontations in the capital city. They earned it by providing security for dignitaries and in efforts to prevent lynchings in North Carolina. They won the respect of prosecutors, judges, jurors, and the public in trials throughout the state by showing their thoroughness in both their case preparation and their investigations of accidents. They then won over the public with their appearance and testimony under cross-examination.

So, you see, I had some big shoes to fill, and I was not going to be the reason the highway patrol failed.

Chief Melvin Hill, Sheriff P.L. Barrow, and almost all of my sergeants and supervisors were good men. Although I did not understand their behavior at times, I did not wish to hurt or damage any of their reputations.

I heard a story about a sergeant I knew that occurred when he was a trooper. I met Sgt. B.W. Parker when he was a line sergeant in Martin County. One day, he was called to a collision and charged the driver with going 70 mph in a 55-mph zone—no radar, no vas-car, and without ever seeing him drive. His speech was unclear when he testified and seemed to mumble his words. When the jury returned, they found the driver guilty. The defense attorney immediately polled the jury, asking each juror for their vote and showing that the jury unanimously agreed that the driver was guilty.

The defense attorney immediately protested, telling the judge he could not understand what Trooper Parker was saying. He did not think the jury was paying attention and felt the verdict was unfair. The judge asked the jury's foreman to explain. His reply was confident: "The defendant ran off the road, struck the ditch, overturned, and came to rest in the field. He had to be going at least 70 mph, and if Mr. Parker said he was going 70. By God, that's how fast he was going."

I wanted my whole career to be like that, where my word was good enough. For nine years, even before I read those words, I practiced being honest and fair as best I could. This book contains stories from my career as a police officer, deputy sheriff, state trooper, and private investigator.

This book describes some of the difficulties I faced and those faced by other law enforcement officers and private investigators today.

I was not unique or more intelligent than anyone else. Through trial and error, I found things that helped me, but the stories in this book demonstrate that it didn't always come easy.

I worked for the Police Department, the Sheriff's Department, the North Carolina Highway Patrol, a civil lawyer, and myself. I sure didn't want to embarrass any of those people. More importantly, I did not want to embarrass people like Jim Winters or Matthew Brinkley, who encouraged this book.

In this book, strong language is used; it is not in any way meant to be offensive. There are racial slurs, but sometimes you have to get in the ditch when you are fighting and use the language the person being arrested uses. I tried. Sometimes, you have to quote exactly what you remember being said. I wish we could speak with less profanity and use fewer racial slurs, but the times and the people we are talking to and dealing with make it necessary to say what was said so you, the reader, feel the exact actions as they happened. Statements made and words used were not softened but appeared as they were spoken and as it was given. Please forgive me for anything that is not civil or does not seem to be what was said. That is how I remember it.

This book includes stories about my family, my life with Sherry, and my boys. These events were significant to me throughout my life, and I want you, the reader, to experience what they were like.

I had little time for family, so remembering these stories brings excitement to a time when there was little family time.

Chapter One: The Early Years

As a youth in Jones County, I remember having a recurring dream. Long before Neil Armstrong did it, I would see two men walking on the moon in my dreams. When the first person caught the second, it became apparent that the second person had done something wrong. When the first person took off his helmet, after seeing the second person, it was always me.

While in high school, I became friends with Roger Smith, a Jones County deputy sheriff. After watching him work, I decided I wanted to be a Police Officer too. The Jones County Sheriff's Department had no policy on ride-a-longs. Ride-a-longs are when a civilian rides with a law enforcement officer. With no policy in effect, Roger let me ride with him. Through Roger, I met Johnny Surles, a North Carolina State Trooper, who would let me ride with him occasionally, too. Because Jones County was away from the District Headquarters, Johnny would get away with it, and if his supervisors didn't know, they didn't care, I guess. Anyway, once I went into Law Enforcement and was sworn in, it became easier to ride along.

Shortly after I started riding with Roger Smith, I was in the sheriff's office one night. Pete Bland, a state Alcohol Law Enforcement Officer who later became Sheriff in Craven County, recruited me to buy some alcohol from a liquor house on the Lenoir County line but inside Jones County. A deputy from Jones County and I went to the home under cover and bought several beers, but when we returned to serve the warrants, there was no alcohol in the place. We felt, and Pete *told us*, that one of the deputies who worked with us had warned the liquor house. That was an experience that I will never forget. I don't know why Pete asked me to make a buy. I had no experience in law enforcement, but maybe he saw something I didn't know was there. It made me think about my desire to become a police officer even more.

I remember working for a friend, Carl Shivar, driving a truck during summer college sessions. He sent me to Pamlico County to retrieve a broken-down truck one day. His brother, Donald Ray, was to go with me. I remember asking Donald Ray who would drive the car back since his license was suspended. He told me he was, and as we went through New Bern, he told me to stop at the ABC store.

When we got to the truck, Donald Ray was so impaired he could hardly stand up, much less drive. He crawled around on the ground, looking up at the engine, but couldn't figure out what was wrong. I frankly doubt that he could even *see* the engine.

Later that night, I found a gun on the ground that must have fallen out of his pocket. When I asked Donald Ray about it, he said, "Yeah, it's mine; when you have enemies like me, you need some protection."

Donald Ray later told me of the time he was shot with a shotgun at Lyman Grant's joint in Kinston, North Carolina. He said that from the time he was able to get up and go home after leaving the hospital, he would break out in a cold sweat when he saw his shotgun hanging on the gun rack in his own home. Anyway, at about 4 a.m., I convinced Donald Ray we could not get the truck running, and I carried him back home.

When we got to his house at the back of Trenton Mill Pond, his brilliant German Shepard Duke ran the opposite way when Donald Ray called him. "Duke, Duke. Come here, Duke," he said. But Duke turned and ran toward Dr. Thompson's trailer. Donald Ray said, "I'll teach you to run," and started shooting toward Duke. He never hit Duke, but he peppered Dr. Thompson's trailer in the morning air while everyone slept.

I yelled, "Got to go," and hurried away before someone called the Sheriff. I remember telling Donald Ray I wanted to go into law enforcement. I remember him telling me not to let my left hand know what my right hand was doing. That was him saying: it's okay, but keep it quiet.

Years later, a friend of mine named Billy Terral, who was a federal alcohol agent, raided a whiskey still that Donald Ray was running. Donald Ray directed Duke to attack Bill. Bill shot and killed Duke and arrested Donald Ray.

I remember when Donald Ray passed away in prison from cirrhosis of the liver. His mother called my mom to invite me to his funeral. I declined, explaining to my mom, "I can't go. He was a convicted murderer, and I work as a state trooper. If I attend his funeral and it becomes known, it could cause problems for me at the highway patrol."

So, I didn't go. Despite this, I always felt that Donald Ray liked me. In my junior year of high school, when it snowed in rural Jones County in eastern North Carolina, there were no cabs, taxis, or buses; you had to drive, find a ride, or walk to get around. I was dating a local girl from Jones County who lived about six miles away. Since it had snowed, there was no school. She had fallen and broken her leg and had surgery. I had not seen her since school was out, so I figured I would drive to her house, but I had no car. When I asked Daddy if I could use his car, he said, "No, not in the snow." I decided I would walk.

I walked about 500 yards from the house when Donald Ray, Sammy Griffin, Ernest Basden, and James Basden came along, stopped, and picked me up. They asked me where I was going, and when I told them, "My girlfriend's house," they said, "Get in." Despite their drinking, they offered me whiskey, but I declined, explaining that I don't drink. They dropped me off at her house and left.

At about 3 o'clock, I decided to head home as it was getting colder. I had six miles to walk, and the snow was not melting. I said goodbye and started walking back home. After about 500 yards, the group picked me up and rode me to my dad's front door. They seemed tired and less energetic this time.

It's worth noting that Donald Ray was sent to prison for

killing a Latino man who spit on him. The man supposedly had a problem with Donald Ray. Donald Ray was said to have just cleared things up. While kind to me, Donald Ray was violent, and I saw him get mad many times over just a little something. It didn't take much to get him upset.

Sammy Griffin shot and killed his wife on the steps of his home. His mother saw what happened, had a heart attack, and died. Sammie was sentenced for murder and is currently in prison.

Ernest Basden was a friend of mine from high school. I liked him because we had attended school together since the first grade. We ran track together, and I would often give him a ride home after track practice since he rode to school with his brother. We were friends, but I lost contact after I went to college and into law enforcement.

After I left Jones County, Ernest got involved with an insurance man's wife, who asked Ernest and his cousin to kill her husband. They did, and Ernest's cousin turned state's evidence against him. Ernest was sentenced to death and was put to death in the state's gas chamber in December 2003. Donald Jacobs, The District Attorney for the 8th Judicial District, became a good friend of mine and prosecuted the case. Jacobs told me Ernest would never be put to death, but before the year ended, the state had executed him. There was one factor against Ernest that hung him. He killed for money. Several other mitigating factors did not relieve that problem.

As far as I know, James Basden was never even arrested. If that is true, he can count his blessings. Not everyone I knew growing up was this violent, but it's just an example to me that I could have quickly gone that way.

Once, I came home with a C on my report card, and Mama asked me, "Who are your friends?" I told her, "Ernest, Bennie, and Ronnie."

She asked me, "Why aren't you friends with Murray, Craig, and Larry?" I said I just wasn't. Mom looked at me and said, "You are as of today." I'm glad she paid attention to that. This is a small example of the attention my mother paid to me. She always watched and ensured I didn't get too far from her guidance.

We did have a federal judge who lived in Trenton, John Larkins. He passed the desegregation rulings down for the eastern district in the '60s and '70s, and that made rural Jones County whites very mad.

One Sunday, right before my high school graduation, I went through Trenton; troopers with shotguns were on each corner around the courthouse block. One of the Troopers I knew was Wesley Oakley, and when I asked him what was going on, he replied, "Someone threatened to kill John Larkins." This seemed to be a call from one person who was upset by a ruling by Judge Larkins and his ruling of desegregation in the late 60s and 70s. Whites in Jones County were upset by these actions and replied violently with both death threats and cross-burnings.

I would go by Judge Larkin's and his wife's home after track practice and talk to them. They were kind to me, particularly when they found out I was a student interested in law enforcement. When I went to East Carolina University, I found out their son-in-law was the business school chair, but I had no interest in that and only talked to him once.

In high school, I was in the first fully integrated classes. One morning, as usual, I went to my locker during my sophomore year, and while there, unbeknownst to me, there was a race riot going on. I was being pelted in the back, and as I turned around, I saw Matthew Brinkley hitting me. Suddenly, I heard Curtis Waters, whom I had known for years, screaming, "You niggers leave him alone!" Curtis, who is Black, worked on the farms putting in tobacco, and we became instant friends working together cropping tobacco.

I was on the 50th-year class reunion committee for our high school class just last year. While I knew Matthew only slightly, we had never been close. One day, at a meeting, Matthew, who is also Black, called me over to his car in the parking lot and told me he had cancer. He asked if I would ensure the reunion went as planned if something should happen to him or if he could not fulfill his duty as leader. I assured him I would, and we became great friends working together throughout the reunion.

Not long after the reunion, Curtis asked me if I had ever told Matthew how I remembered the day of the riots. I told Curtis that was 50 years ago, and why should I bring it up now? We are different people and have different opinions about the world than in 1971 and 1972.

Matthew, Curtis, and I have become like brothers. I gladly welcome both into my home; honestly, if I do anything, I enjoy doing it with them.

We spoke recently about hate, and we all feel that, as the song goes, God blesses little children while they are still too young to hate. Children don't usually know hate. They gladly play together, and it's only after they are grown and they see how others treat people who are different from them that they learn to hate. While I was surrounded by hatred all my life, not from my parents but from people in my life, I have tried not to learn any hatred, whether it be toward Blacks, Gays, or others. These friends of mine have helped me with this, and to say I love them would be an understatement.

Because I have tried to live my life free of hatred, and I hope it rubbed off on my sons and relatives. I saw the dignity Curtis, Matt, and all the Blacks who worked for my friends and family on the farms had. I know they handled indignity with grace and class. From eating on the porch away from the Whites to tolerating bugs and flies on that porch as if they were beneath us in worth. I now hope I never have to face that indignity myself because I may never be as kind to Whites now as the Blacks were to us then.

Chapter Two: Looking for D. B. Cooper

1971, halfway around the world, a man named Dan Cooper, or DB Cooper, bought a one-way ticket for flight #305 from Portland, Oregon, to Seattle, Washington.

During the flight, the quiet man in his forties, wearing a business suit and black tie with a white shirt, ordered a bourbon and soda while the flight awaited takeoff. At about 3 p.m., he handed the stewardess a note indicating that a bomb was in his briefcase and asked her to sit with him. She did as she was told, and he opened the suitcase, showed her a bundle of wires and red colored sticks, and asked her to write down what he had told her.

Cooper demanded $200,000 in $20 bills and four parachutes.

When the plane landed in Seattle, Washington, the thirty-six passengers and four parachutes were exchanged for the demanded money. However, Cooper ordered several crew members to remain on board and changed the flight route to Mexico City. Still, somewhere between Seattle, Washington, and Reno, Nevada, Cooper jumped out the back of the plane with a parachute and the money. Cooper was never found, but some of the money was, and there was much discussion about who Dan Cooper was. About five months later, a similar thing happened over the skies of Colorado.

Immediately after takeoff, a male passenger was seen holding a hand grenade. The stewardess was given detailed instructions on who was allowed near the plane and the course they were to take. $ 500,000 and four parachutes were asked for. Five hours after the altercation started, a stewardess realized the man had jumped.

Salt Lake City FBI offices received a tip from a concerned citizen who said that Richard Floyd McCoy Jr., a Vietnam veteran, helicopter pilot, and avid and capable skydiver, had told his friend of a foolproof plan to escape capture. McCoy was a Utah Air National Guard member and a police science major at Brigham Young University. Evidence was gathered about him, which led to an arrest order.

McCoy was taken into custody, and a search of his home found all of the $500,000 except $30, along with the electric typewriter with keys that matched the hijacker's notes. $30 was just about the amount to fill a gas tank in 1971. McCoy was tried and sentenced to forty-five years in a federal prison in Pennsylvania.

Two years later, McCoy and three of his fellow inmates hijacked a garbage truck at the Lewisburg Federal Prison in Pennsylvania and escaped.

All the above information was taken from the news reports of 1971 and the Cooper incident and is verified if researched.

Within months of the escapes, my cousin Maggie Small, the only woman I knew at the time who served as a police chief in North Carolina, was on duty in Trenton. Maggie was the Chief, and her husband Dewey was the Assistant Chief. They took turns patrolling during the week and worked together on weekends. Dewey had the day off. She and Trooper Fred Sullivan of the North Carolina Highway Patrol were parked at the gas station across from the Jones County Courthouse, talking to each other while both were on duty. It was nearly 10 p.m., and Fred was due to get off duty at 10 p.m. Maggie saw a Lincoln Continental pull into the parking lane, drive past the Branch Bank and Trust, and down to the stop light at NC 58. It turned south, going toward Pollocksville. Trenton had only two police officers at the time.

Maggie told Fred she needed to check the car. Fred replied that he was due to get off at 10 p.m. and did not want to check on anyone else that night. The fact that Fred didn't agree to stop that car probably saved both of their lives.

The next day, the four escapees robbed the bank in

Pollocksville. They went to the Bell Farm, about three miles from the bank. Mr. Bell owned a small airplane and kept it on the farm. Mr. Bell saw the four escapees and notified the police, who captured two of them. Only Melvin Dale Walker and Richard Floyd McCoy Jr. escaped.

I started working at Snow Hill in August 1974, my first job in law enforcement due to my age. As a young officer, I wanted all the experience I could get. I had planned to ride with Johnny Surles that night. When I arrived at the Jones County Courthouse, Johnny informed me that we had to go to a spot in Jones County near Cove City and look for Richard Floyd McCoy Jr., one of the men who had robbed the Pollocksville bank that day.

We arrived at the location and met several deputies and other troopers, and together we started checking cars.

Shortly after we arrived, a woman came up, and Johnny Surles told her he had to check her trunk. She asked him what he was looking for. He told her we were looking for a man named Richard Floyd McCoy, Jr. from Cove City, who had robbed the bank in Pollocksville. Standing at the rear of her car, I could hear some conversation between the two, but not everything. She replied, "He's my husband, and I hope you don't catch him."

Within a few months, McCoy had been killed in a shootout in Virginia Beach, Virginia, with the FBI, and Walker had been captured.

Years later, after McCoy's wife and mother had died, his two children admitted that he was Dan Cooper, and both his wife and his mother were involved in his escape. The children said they had remained quiet to protect the mother and grandmother; both were accomplices in the crimes.

Chapter Three: Living in Snow Hill

When I started in law enforcement, I was just twenty years old and a kid. Living in Snow Hill, I began to grow up while working in law enforcement. I took every opportunity I could to learn more about the actual law and how best to control the situations I encountered. I often practiced what I would do in any situation, like a black belt in karate repeating a move to learn it.

I made many mistakes before and after becoming a police officer. This book should not give the impression that I did everything right.

Before I met Melvin Hill, Snow Hill Police Chief, I met his son-in-law, Henry Epps. I worked for the summer between college sessions at Frosty Morn Packing Company in Kinston, where I met Henry. When I told Henry I was looking for a job in law enforcement, he suggested I speak with his father-in-law, Melvin Hill.

The following weekend, I drove to Snow Hill and met Melvin. Later, when I returned for my interview, Melvin asked me if I had ever done anything illegal. I'm sure I had, but the big thing that stood out to me was the freshest in my mind.

One night, about a year earlier, I went with several guys from my university to a local golf course and took some golf ball washers and flags off the course. I had to be crazy. I parked my car next to a dorm where I was a student. The trunk was raised, and the washers were visible. No one questioned my right to have them; even when I drove home with my trunk raised and the flags blowing in the wind, I had no problems. I just prayed that once I told Melvin about my escapade, he would not arrest me, and he would forgive me and grant me a job.

God must have heard my prayers because Melvin told me

it was a fraternity prank. He told me to go deep in the woods and dispose of them, which I gladly did as soon as I returned home.

Melvin Hill was a retired game warden who was a good teacher and leader. Shortly after his retirement, he became chief of Police in Snow Hill. He grew up in an orphanage and often told me how tough it had been. He was a Mason, which encouraged me to become a person of high integrity, even though I probably fell short at times. Melvin and my father-in-law even drove up to Gates County while I was there to raise me in the lodge. Being raised in the lodge refers to the lodge's membership process.

The police department and the town hall were in an office across the street from the courthouse. I could look out the door and see the courthouse on the hill. One day, Melvin told me this story, which stayed with me: "If you're over there in that jail, at the top of the courthouse, charged with a crime, I might be able to help you. We have a medical examiner here named Sandy Rouse; if you're lying on his slab dead, there just ain't one damn thing I can do for you, boy."

Melvin used the story of Sandy's slab to impress the need for me to stay alive, which stuck with me.

I got to know Sandy Rouse better over the next two years. He would get the bodies in from auto accidents and murders. I watched as Sandy checked each one with his rubber gloves on, poking and prodding to see where their significant injury was. Then he would look at me while taking off the gloves and say, "Let's go get a hot dog."

Years later, I met an embalmer in Gates County named John Katuniack, who embalmed for David Twiford at Twiford Funeral Homes in Elizabeth City. John had the same ritual as Sandy. He would poke and prod, looking for the injury, and then remove his gloves. Without any sense of grief, he would say, "Let's go get a hotdog." I found out later that John knew Sandy and had worked for him.

The connection of the story Melvin gave me, along with the

work and behaviors of Sandy and John, showed me that I must remove any sympathy or grief as I work and retain it. This altered my behavior in judgment and would possibly prevent me from getting killed.

My first DWI arrest came as I stood at the intersection in front of the courthouse. I was flagged down while walking the streets and was informed about a car driving erratically. I went to the intersection and saw the car coming. The vehicle stopped at the light, and I walked onto the street; I noticed the driver was impaired. I placed him under arrest and moved his car to the shoulder. I placed him under arrest while Melvin stood by with the driver and then walked him upstairs to the jail, where the breathalyzer was located. Any protest by the driver would have been useless since I was legally authorized to make the arrest and had Probable Cause. He checked over .10 on the breathalyzer and was convicted in court of driving impaired. A .10 on the breathalyzer is all that was needed to convict as the law required a .10 impairment, regardless of physical or mental impairment. Today, it's a .08, which is even lower.

While a police officer in Snow Hill, I was paid under Green Lamp, a program for needy people in Greene and Lenoir Counties. While that hurt my pride, I realized it helped the town put another officer on the streets. Since I was in college, it also offered me a job, some money, and a chance to grow.

My first Christmas in Snow Hill, we hung a Christmas wreath on the door. One day, a sanitation worker walked into the office, looking and acting like Fat Albert, the comic character. He first looked at Melvin sitting behind his desk and then at the wreath on the door and asked most sincerely, "Who died?"

Melvin was agitated that day about something and looked up from his work and said, "It's Christmas, you dumbass." Sensing Melvin's anger, the sanitation worker left us alone at the town hall.

I was only 20 years old and weighed only 130 pounds,

soaking wet. The uniform pants I got were much too big; even when hemmed, I found my rear pockets touched. Most young officers spend much time in altercations with arrestees, so I asked the Chief how we would help me gain weight, and he said, "We're going to feed you biscuits." He did, and over the years, I bloomed to 260 pounds, though I eventually lost forty. Of course, 260 slows you down and also creates health problems for the body, which I had some fifty years later.

I walked the streets and patrolled daily, growing in skills and knowledge and making friends in Greene County.

One day, I went to work at 6 a.m. Deputy Sheriff Len Edwards came to me and asked if I was from Jones County. I said I was, and he asked if I would go with him to where two brothers, who had raped a girl in Greene County, had fled to Lenoir County just north of the Jones County line. Since I was familiar with the area and could assist him with what might be out of place. Besides, one more pair of eyes could never hurt.

I left, and although I should have called the chief, I didn't. I went to Lenoir County, where the Chief Deputy, Early Whaley, awaited. He informed me that the two brothers, after raping the girl, had fled to a field and jumped from their car, running across that field into the woods. They had returned to their cousin's home about a mile away, asking her to take them to Greenville. She did, though, having no idea they had raped the girl. The cousin only thought their vehicle had died, and they needed a ride to get home.

She led us to the mobile home in a trailer park in Greenville. We entered the house and found the two boys lying on the bed, unconscious. Both were handcuffed and arrested without incident.

When we returned to Snow Hill, I became even more impressed with Sheriff P.L. Barrow. While I did not work for him, he was the Sheriff of the county and the top Law Enforcement officer in Greene County.

BRONNIE QUINN

The girl, who was black, had been raped by two white boys, and a delegation of about 30 Black men gathered outside the courthouse.

I was told they were there to hang the boys. The Sheriff advised me to remain with some of his deputies outside his office. In about 45 minutes, the delegation left, and the Sheriff appeared confident he had satisfied them. The girl would get justice, and in a few months, they both were given hefty prison sentences for rape.

Although I probably did not follow the procedure, the Chief supported my decision to leave town. The Sheriff seemed willing to help me if I had any problems. I have no doubt that had it not been for that trip to assist the other deputies, the Sheriff would have never invited me to work for him within just a few months.

Once, while working radar in Snow Hill, I got into a chase that led me to a place I had never been before. Ricky Whaley, the oldest son of Chief Deputy Early Whaley, was riding with me one night when a car came through at a high rate of speed in a 35mph zone.

I activated my blue light and siren and followed the car, but the driver refused to stop. I followed him while Ricky, who had delivered newspapers down this roadway, told me where every curve and bump in the road was. After following him for about 20 miles, the driver turned down a dirt road and overturned in the curve in Lenoir County.

I exited the patrol car, snatched up the driver, and wasted no force apprehending him. Then, I called for the rescue of the passenger.

Both men went to the hospital in Kinston, and when I arrived, I found that the driver was actually in worse shape than the passenger. Of course, I had shown no mercy to the driver, thinking he was not injured at all.

Tires were worn down, and the cost of operation fees had to be considered, but the chief only gave me a warning. This was just another example of how things changed so fast in law enforcement. One day you're working on a story

23

of rape, and the next, you're after people for speeding who refuse to stop.

1974, when Richard Nixon stepped down from the Presidency, I was with the Sheriff, the Chief, and Superior Court Judge Robert Rouse of Farmville, eating lunch at the Blue Ram Restaurant just outside Snow Hill. Superior Court Judges are the closest thing to God in law enforcement, and hardly anyone ever questions their authority. They have almost complete jurisdiction in their courts and demand total respect. Usually, they are older and more politically experienced because of their experiences in law and because they have a more extensive jurisdiction with their base of politics. They have complete authority to pronounce death sentences and to send people to prison, usually without lengthy appeals.

I was not that familiar with politics and just knew that Nixon had kept me from going to Vietnam by ending the war. Judge Rouse, Sheriff Barrow, and Chief Hill were all Democrats and were talking about Richard Nixon, a Republican who had just resigned from the Presidency the day before. I just interjected and spoke without thinking, "He kept me from Vietnam, and I like him."

Immediately, the Chief kicked me under the table, and I guess I must have screamed. Judge Rouse just shook his head. Later that day, when I went home, I spoke with my dad, who knew Judge Rouse. Dad advised me to get with Judge Rouse and apologize.

I met the judge at the courthouse door the next day and apologized for my idiotic behavior. It was ridiculous for three reasons.

1. Law Enforcement is a paramilitary organization whose members do not speak openly about their politics. The public needed to be secure in the belief that I would do my job regardless of my likes or dislikes of a person.

2. They all thought I was too inexperienced to have developed an opinion, and they certainly did not

want to hear it, even if I did.

3. My daddy told me too.

Rouse was very polite and said something I will remember as long as I live: "You might feel that way, but your children and grandchildren may not."

That was before I knew about Nixon's secret hit list and his violations of our Constitution. I now think Judge Rouse was right. Had it not been for our hands-off treatment of Nixon in 1974, when Gerald Ford granted him a pardon for those crimes, we would not have had to deal with Donald Trump in 2020 and all the charges he now faces. I still believe that no one in America should be above the law, even Presidents.

I remember Bob Chamberlain and Paul Frazelle drinking wine in the alley behind Harry's Restaurant. I remember how Bob Chamberlain looked like a person who had developed cancer scores on his lips. Paul and Bob would sip a drink of wine and then pass the bottle to each other. Paul's dad had been a Superior Court Judge, and Paul objected when I took his wine, saying, "There is nothing wrong with wine, Jesus Christ, drunk wine," and that's when Johnny Watkins, another officer I had recruited from East Carolina, where we both were students said, "yes, but he didn't live but 32 years. Both were alcoholics that we had to deal with every day, but who usually were not so noticeable in their drinking in a public place.

One Christmas, the Town of Snow Hill had its holiday parade after dark. Doll Joyner was assigned a shovel and told to follow the horses and remove the manure they dropped. I don't know what they paid him, but it wasn't enough for me to have done it. Doll was another of the town alcoholics, but while he was drunk most of the time, there wasn't any evil or aggression in Doll at all. He was always smiling and thankful. I always felt that if given a chance to cure himself of alcohol, Doll would take it. I never found out for sure, but that was my belief.

One day in 1976, I had lunch at about 2 p.m., well after

the regular meal hour. Snow Hill had a barbeque house on Kingold Blvd. run by a little black man named William Randolph. William had a room for white people and a room for blacks. Since this was 1976, I figured segregation was over. Since I did not want to eat alone and no one was in the white's room, I went to the blacks' room.

I ordered a barbeque sandwich and a Coke and waited at the bar. Suddenly, I heard a terrible fuss coming from the kitchen. "Did you tell him?" He asked." Did you tell him?" He asked. " Did you tell him? " He asked. "I told him, I told him!"

Suddenly, William walked out. Now, William Randolph was portly, to be friendly, and about 5'4" tall. He looked at me and spoke, "Mr. Quinn, white folks eat over there. Black folks eat over here." I just replied, "William, I don't care. I want to eat and not be alone." I ate my sandwich, drank my Coke, and returned to work.

One night before I left the police department, I was called to Harry's restaurant on Main Street, where some teens had thrown pumpkins into the restaurant. The owner was a Lebanese gentleman who was quite upset. "My restaurant, they destroyed my restaurant. What are you going to do about my restaurant?" he said in a Lebanese dialect accent.

A crowd of teens were standing around laughing about the joke. I made a decision that needed to be perceived as more legally binding. So I dug deep. While it was not based on legal application, it sure sounded good. I called for martial law and told the teens that anyone on the streets in 20 minutes would be arrested. The streets became empty. I should have mentioned that the Governor was the only person who could call for martial law, but it got the job done anyway.

In Spring 1975, on a Saturday night, I was working traffic on Kingold Blvd. around 10 pm when I saw a car traveling east with a headlight out. I stopped the car and saw the prettiest girl, about 21, get out. I asked her for her license but can't tell you her name today. We talked, and she didn't seem like anyone I had ever met. She was relaxed, and we spoke about her light being out in her car. I told her to get it fixed since the town had no written warning books and because it was not a substantial violation of the law. She was from Snow Hill and asked me when I got off work. I told her 12, and we went our separate ways.

At 12, I pulled onto the street across from the Town Hall to park the cruiser, and there she sat on the brick wall around the courthouse, which joins the street across from the town Hall.

I gave the car keys to the officer who was already there to replace me and told him I had a visitor and was leaving. He acknowledged the information, and the girl and I left to drive where I stayed. The girl and I left together and went to Mrs. Albritton's house, where I got a change of clothes. With her driving and me changing clothes, we headed to the Holiday Inn in Kinston.

I did not have the money for a room, but I did have a Gulf Credit Card that I used to buy gas, and with that credit card, I got the room. We went inside, and from that point on, we had sex on and off all night except when we had a conversation, which, to be honest, was sparse.

Around 5 am, I decided to take her back to Snow Hill. Since my dad usually passed by the motel in the mornings, he might see my car, and I would need help explaining this, so we took off.

As we entered Snow Hill, I asked her, "Say you left your husband?" She said, "Yes." When I asked, "Saturday,"

During the night, she mentioned briefly that she had once been married but had left him; I thought asking her "when" in general conversation was necessary. Her reply floored me because it meant that she had left him the day before we had sex, and they were still married.

I'm old-fashioned, and in my mind, if you were unfaithful to him, you would be unfaithful to me. That pretty well ended any serious relationship we might have had. I was single, and while this was months before I met my wife, it still haunts me.

About two years later, I worked with the Sheriff and went to the Magistrate's Office to get a warrant. When I walked in, guess who was standing there?

Both she and her husband were standing there, having gotten a ticket or received a warrant for a worthless check or something of a legal nature. Her husband was discussing it with the magistrate. She stood behind her husband, waving at me and throwing me kisses, which I waved off and shook my head as if to say "no." I couldn't stand it, and I walked out the door. I almost ran out of the building to my car and drove out of town until I felt safe. When I stopped, I took deep breaths and finally relaxed. I never saw her again and never wanted to

When the Sheriff approached the County Commissioners about hiring me, he told me it was the easiest thing he had ever asked them for. Over those two years in Snow Hill, the men on the county commissioner's board became friends of mine. They all knew me well and respected me.

The Commissioner's Chairman was a close friend whom I introduced to his future son-in-law, and we were very close.

I worked in the Snow Hill Police Department for two years. It was the best two years of my life up to that point. I met so many people from all over Greene County, including members of the Highway Patrol, and those were the people I wanted to emulate.

One person I met early on was Sergeant Lewis Taylor, who, unless things changed, would have to investigate me if I applied to the Highway Patrol, and he ultimately did.

I met and worked with old and new friends in the Police Department. I was around Troopers Jim Crumpler and Pat Whitehurst, my old friends and the husband of my third-grade schoolteacher, Wesley Oakley.

Crumpler called me Tiger, and I liked him. Pat was promoted to Line Sergeant after I got to Gates County and became my direct supervisor there.

I rented a room from Mrs. Albritton, a retired schoolteacher whose husband was a wealthy farmer who had passed away. When I asked her about renting the room, she told me it was $50 a month and no meals would be provided, to which I agreed.

About two weeks after I moved in, I walked into the living room, and she told me dinner would be prepared in about 15 minutes. From then on, I ate dinner with her each night.

I walked in earlier than expected one evening, probably the first Christmas I was there. Mrs. Albritton and three other women were sitting around the kitchen table with cards and a whiskey bottle on the table. Mrs. Albritton looked at me as I entered the room and said, "Oops, you caught us." Southern ladies never drank in public, and Mrs. Albritten was a Southern lady. She was about 80 at the time and wanted her reputation intact. Along with the others, who were all at least 80 years old, they were very Victorian.

Snow Hill became my home away from my actual home in Jones County. Only about 50 miles separated me from home, but it seemed like hundreds of miles. To be truthful, Snow Hill was the only home I needed at the time, but it was also all the home I wanted. I was happy to see my family occasionally when I wasn't working in Snow Hill.

After Johnny Watkins, a friend and fellow student from East Carolina, came on board. One Sunday, I got information about a house in Snow Hill where two guys lived. The guys sold some pot to a person who had informed against them. After getting the information, I quickly got a warrant, and Johnny and I served it. When we did, we found the pot, although not much, and while we were there, the owner of the property, a little older lady, Mrs. Edwards, came in. She asked what we were doing. One of us, Johnny or myself, told her we were serving a warrant. She looked at the two boys and told them to leave when they finished with me. At that point, Johnny called her over to the side of the room and asked if she would rent the building to him, and she did. The very next week after they left, Johnny moved in.

Chapter Four: Working as Greene County Deputy

Switching from the Police Department to the Sheriff's department gave me many opportunities to learn more about the law. I had to handle civil and criminal cases, and most importantly, I had to learn when to act and when not to act.

The first thing I had to learn was that my actions could be used against me and against the person who hired me. I owed my job to the Sheriff and was indebted to him.

Right after I went to the Sheriff's Department, the County, represented by the Sheriff, bought me a 1974 Plymouth 440 Magnum to work with. Man, would it fly? One night, I drove the 10 miles from Walstonburg to Snow Hill in just 5 minutes. I had never experienced this kind of speed before. I reached speeds of 145 MPH, and like I said, I had never gone that fast before, even in a city police car.

I remember leaving the sheriff's office and going south on NC 58 one evening at about 6 p.m. in a 35 MPH zone. I was traveling about 70 MPH when I met the Sheriff in his patrol car. He didn't call or say anything to me, but the next day, as usual, he was at the courthouse. When he saw me, he asked me to go to the jail at the top of the courthouse. I knew something was up.

He shut the wire screen door as he entered the elevator behind me. The Sheriff was a tall country-type fellow who chewed cigars because he could not smoke them. He had experienced a heart condition years before, and while he was a calm man, he could get excited, so I did not want him upset with me.

As we went up in the elevator, he took his cigar out of his teeth and faced me with his 6-foot-tall frame, all 230 pounds. Looking down at me, he said in his local dialect, "Yestidy, when I seen you, you was in a hurry, weren't you?"

All I could think of was lying, so I did. "Sheriff, I had someone who was going to give me some information on a drug sale, and I was late," I said. He lowered his head and replied personally, "I guess I'll have to buy you a tricycle." His meaning was clear: "Knock it off or look for another job," so I immediately chose the former.

The Sheriff was good to me in many ways. He chose me when he needed someone to travel to Camp Lejeune and pick up Marines who had yet to pay off their tickets. He even let me go on Monday evenings and stay with my parents in Jones County. On Tuesday, I would go to the Provost Marshal's office. When I was done, I could return to Mom and Dad's home and stay with them until Wednesday. Then, I returned the money from the Marines to the Clerk of Court.

On one trip, I was allowed to attend a Provost Martial hearing against a Marine who was accused of trying to take an M-16 rifle through the front gate and off the base. I was also allowed to visit the Marine dogs, see them work, and go to the officer's lunchroom, where only Marine officers were fed.

On another occasion, I got to the base at 9 AM, and a young Marine entered the cubicle the Marine Corps had set up for me. He told me he had no money and would have to return to Snow Hill with me as my prisoner. I explained to him that I had spent the night before with my parents and would spend that night with them. I told him I was leaving at 3 pm and that he should find the $16.00 court cost to end the matter. If he didn't get the money, he would have to go with me, and I was going to sleep at Mom's house, but he would be sleeping in the trunk of my car. Then, I asked if he understood, and he replied that he did and left.

He entered about two minutes before 3 p.m., waiving the $16.00. He asked me if I knew where he got the money, and I told him I didn't care. He replied, "I got it from a loan shark." The $16.00 probably cost him $60.00 from a loan shark. I took his $16.00 and gave him a receipt, and frankly, I just tried to forget him, but for some reason, he has remained with me. I regret my attitude. That night, I stayed at Dad's house and returned to Snow Hill the next day.

Sometimes, the Sheriff would allow me to fly in the State Bureau of Investigation Helicopter, spotting marijuana patches. Although I wouldn't say I like to fly today, I took every opportunity to get in the air as a young man. Flying in the Bureau's Chopper was also fun. The pilot took me all over the county looking for patches of marijuana. When we saw what might be a patch, I would radio the information to a team on the ground that would look for the patch.

The Sheriff also allowed me to drive him in parades whenever my town had them, which I enjoyed. We were always the first car to lead the parade.

I remember that the Sheriff would get me to drive him in my patrol car around the county when an election was approaching. As I was driving, he would direct me to pull into a store or business establishment. When the owner or proprietor came out to the car, he would hold up a list of names and say, "Oh, this here fellow, we don't need him, but this here fellow we need bad. You understand?" They would agree, and the sheriff would motion for me to proceed. We went all over the county to people who had supported him, and he told them he needed the names on that list to do his job that much easier. People running for Judge and county commissioner were on that list, and all were Democrats.

Everything was not always good, and I guess life is that way. I had to view suicides and murders. Rapes and robberies. I investigated everything I was called to. We didn't have investigators, so each deputy investigated their cases.

I was remembering the girl that was raped when I was in Snow Hill. She was a beautiful young woman. I felt so bad when, one day, she was at a club in Maury, and a man came out and saw someone he was upset with. He suddenly yelled, "There is the SOB now!" and pulled a gun, firing and striking the girl in the head, killing her. I went

33

to the club, which was a mess. People were everywhere.

The next day, I went with Early Whaley to Chapel Hill to the Medical Examiner's office, where an autopsy was conducted.

Bodies were being autopsied on several tables that day. I'll never forget the smell and the way she was autopsied. Inside the morgue was a stump with no legs, hands, or head, and they were having trouble identifying that body.

First, her chest was cut directly under the breast, and her breasts were folded back over her face and hooked on her chin. Her organs were examined to determine if she had any reason to die other than the wound, which was quickly found to be negative. Then her head was cut like a pumpkin on the rear, and her brain was raked out in a cup and weighed. The bullet was removed and given to me, and I was charged with keeping and retaining it until court. The whole experience was draining, and I was glad to have it behind me.

A similar case happened off NC 58 one day when a prostitute from Fayetteville was visiting a married man. His wife came home, and the wife shot the prostitute while she stood at the door. I had to retrieve the bullet that had lodged in her cervix. But this time, the victim didn't die, and the surgeon at the hospital placed it in a cup and brought it to me.

When we went to court, the prostitute told the judge she made good money and had been out of work for several months. The judge asked her if she knew prostitution was illegal in North Carolina. Then he told her to contact the windows and doors office in Washington, DC, for reimbursement. He was being factious because the Bureau of Windows and Doors does not exist. The judge was tired of arguing with an uneducated person who acted like a fool. He put a small fine on the shooter, who admitted guilt and moved on.

In 1976 and 1977, Greene County was more like Andy and Mayberry RFD than New York Crimes, and life was laid-back. Don't get me wrong; we had our share of killings and robberies, but most were crimes of passion, or people needed money and were committing robbery to live. Many people in that county at that time might have hit you, but they ensured you were already down when they did.

One night, after I started working for the Sheriff, I discovered what pure, unadulterated evil was. A guy walked into a local Quick Mart on North Harper Street and robbed it. When he ran out, the owner ran out behind him, shooting. Although he didn't hit the robber, he busted out his window. Little identification was given for the robber; honestly, we had little to go on.

A few months passed, and the crook must have thought Greene County was easy pickings, so he hit another store. This time, he hit a store owned by Chief Deputy Early Whaley. Although we didn't get him, Whaley located enough evidence to give to other officers. With that information, the officers began looking for that type of car and that particular individual. Then they found him. Fayetteville police spotted the vehicle, and the man ran. They chased him, and he was blocked in by a train crossing and arrested there. Two Deputies transferred him back to Greene County and locked him away at the top of the Greene County Courthouse to stew and await trial.

In 1976-77, inmates made calls using telephones. The inmate was taken unhandcuffed to the phone in an area at the top of the courthouse adjacent to the jail, where they made their calls and returned to the cell, usually with no problem at all.

The robber asked Ben Albritton, who was running the dispatch that day, to take him to the phone, and Ben obliged him. Ben was a Road Deputy and should have known the man could be dangerous. Still, he completely ignored or forgot this individual's criminality.

At any rate, after making his call, Ben went to put the man back in his cell when he attacked Ben, pushing him into the cell and knocking Ben to the floor. The prisoner then ran towards the elevator, down to the deputy's room, and exited the courthouse.

Of course, when Ben finally regained his senses, he ran downstairs and called for help on the radio, and we all came running. The prisoner had run out of the courthouse and into the Contentnea Creek woods, which ran east and west away from the courthouse.

Within minutes, we were all looking for him. Even private citizens approached our checking stations on the roads leading out of town with guns. They were ready to do justice to this criminal. But he escaped by catching a ride or hiding until we were gone. Since we knew who he was, he was a lot easier to find. Fayetteville police knew him and arrested him. When he got back in Wayne County, the Sheriff adjusted his confinement. He was shipped straight to Central Prison and put into their maximum-security unit to await trial.

Changes were also made in the phone process. This time, a cell phone was given to the inmate to make the call, but the inmate was never removed from the cell until trial. Then, two deputies went to remove him and escort him.

The prisoner was brought back to the county for court, and because his behavior was so profane, the judge ordered him to be gagged and handcuffed before trial. He got a hefty prison sentence and was not allowed to speak while getting it.

On one occasion, I was called to a shooting outside Hookerton where a man and his wife were constantly at each other's throats. On this one occasion, the man had just tired, I guess, of the constant arguments and shot his wife, or maybe the anger just got the best of him. When we arrived, he was taken into custody. His defense was not that he had not shot her but that he had shot over her, and she jumped up. It wouldn't have held water, but that was an original idea.

With the daddy in prison and the mother in the grave, the in-laws fought for the custody of the children; friendly in-laws went for the others' throats to gain custody of those kids. Since all the children were under 16 years of age, they needed a guardian, and the court had to appoint someone. So, the grandparents became the logical choice, but the issue was which ones.

One thing I had to do as a deputy was fight all the time. Often, I was the only deputy working. There were only nine road deputies for the county, approximately 266 miles in total, and since some were in court and on case investigation many times, I had to work alone.

I remember stopping a car one night near Lizzie, and a guy came out of the passenger side. Frankly, I don't remember his name, and it doesn't matter. I told him to get back inside and tell the driver to exit. As he crossed over from the passenger side to the driver's side door, I realized who he was, but once he exited the car, he went into a karate stance and lunged toward me. I struck him in the head with my flashlight, and we both fell to the ground. As I looked up, I saw people - young men running towards me. I remember saying, "Lord, I'm coming home!" They, instead of attacking me, grabbed the passenger, handcuffed him, and placed him in my patrol car. The young men were his cousins, and they were upset that he was acting foolishly.

On the way back to the Courthouse, I started to turn into the courthouse parking lot and saw through my peripheral vision that he had slipped under the seat belt and prepared to kick me with his feet. I reacted by slapping him. I remember his head banging off the passenger window. The sound was like a Bugs Bunny movie. "bo—ng."

Once inside, I called a trooper, a certified breath test operator, to administer a chemical sobriety test. Wesley Oakley was assigned, and he and I were soon busy filling out the forms to document the man's impairment.

Suddenly, I heard a slap, turned, and saw a man standing over the arrested person. It was his dad. Looking down at the youth on the floor, he said, "Son, you don't talk that way to me." After that, he took the breathalyzer test, and the results exceeded the legal limit.

About a week later, I stopped the same youth again, not knowing it was him, for weaving in his lane. His head was wrapped up like a mummy, but his attitude was, "Yes, sir," and "No, sir."

I remember the judge at his hearing was Herbert Hardy, who had become a good friend of mine. Herbert looked at the boy standing at the defense table with his lawyer, Donald Pollock. Pollock told the judge, "Your honor, Mr. Quinn, beat my client worse than Mohamed Ali beat George Foreman."

Judge Hardy looked at him and said, "Son, you come back before me; you better bring your toothbrush; you're going away from here, do you understand? Fight my officers? I will not tolerate that, no sir. You hear me?" Herbert Hardy liked me, and I often went by his home. We would spend hours just talking, which made it easier for him to be harder on anyone I was fighting when we went to court because he knew me well.

Donald Pollock was a black lawyer from Kinston who was every bit 6 foot five inches tall and just as polite and friendly as anyone would want. Each time I sat opposite him, it was usually a case where I had to fight to arrest someone. I usually hit them pretty hard, but Donald knew I would not have been fighting if they had just listened to what I told them. Pollock always acted at least as if his clients were dead wrong, even though he represented them well. Representation did not mean he got them off, but he knew that. He only had to get them as light a sentence as possible. Sparing them from Draconian sentences was a skill only a few lawyers learned. Donald Pollock was one of the best.

Herbert Hardy was a typical judge who was quite a politician. His son Steve was a beach music DJ, and Steve and I became good friends. Herbert would be on the streets in Snow Hill, Kinston, or Goldsboro, wherever he was holding court, shaking hands before court started, many times by 7 AM. However, when he got on the bench, he was Judge Hardy, and you'd better listen to him.

One day, a friend of mine, Trooper Ben Fleming, wrote three people tickets for passing on yellow lines in the Brown Town community of Greene County on Highway 58.

Herbert called Ben to the bench and said, "Ben, these two fellows are good Greene County blue blood, and they contribute to my campaign each time I run, so I am going to find them not guilty." Ben asked if he wanted him to testify, and Herbert said, "Yes, tell it like it was, and I'm going to find them not guilty." Ben told the story of how he saw these two men of Greene County, both reputable farmers, passing on a yellow line; their names are unimportant today. Then, Herbert found each not guilty, but the third man was a truck driver from out of state, and he found him guilty and threw the book at him. WAS HE FAIR? PROBABLY NOT, BUT WAS HE A POLITICIAN? SURE.

All judges are politicians first because without being supported by local people, they can't get the money or support to run for office. Herbert passed away 45 years ago, but things have not changed in the world. It would be nice to assume that friendships and money play no part in justice, but it does, just like Clarence Thomas, who sits on the Supreme Court today and receives gifts valued in the millions of dollars. We argue about ethics and the need for reform there. So yes, there is a need, but it's nothing new, and people have done it for generations, so Herbert was not alone in his behavior.

One night taught me just how dangerous law enforcement is.

Whaley and I were on patrol in the county. We were the only ones working, so we checked stores and business doors around the county. As we entered the Ormondsville Community, Whaley, who knew the businesses, noticed that a door between the grocery store and the service station was open. According to him, it was supposed to be closed. As we exited the car and went to the store, I saw a giant gun pointed at my head through the glass on the front of the building as I was walking just feet from the window. The barrel looked like a cannon. Whaley recognized the owner and called to him. The man lowered his gun.

The business had been broken into several times, and the owner had been sleeping inside to catch the thieves. I realized just how close I was to dying when I left that night, and I also learned a valuable lesson. *Don't rush in, look, and take your time.*

Most of the time, I felt like I was making a difference in the world, but a few times, I felt helpless.

One such case occurred when I had to investigate and charge a 17-year-old boy who was with his friends when they robbed a store. Two of the boys went inside a store and robbed it at gunpoint. They told the 17-year-old what they'd done when they returned to the car. When he got home, he did nothing. He didn't call the police. He didn't attempt to inform the police in any way. He remained mute to the authorities, and this behavior made him as guilty of robbery as the ones who entered the store and pulled a gun on the owner. Under the law, when one person commits a felony and is aided by another, the second person is guilty of the crime like the first. It's called aiding and abetting, and what the 17-year-old did was aid and abet a felony robbery, so much so that he received seven years in prison, which was also the minimum sentence for armed robbery in North Carolina at that time.

Another case involved a 17-year-old boy who went out with a young girl, and they had sex. He was charged with rape but told me in a most sincere way that it was not rape. He claimed she allowed the sex but only after returning home cried rape to her parents once they began pressuring her. Nevertheless, he was convicted and pulled time in prison for rape.

A similar story happened in Maury when a merchant I knew called me and told me his daughter had been raped. She was 14 years old at the time. I went to the home and found the man sitting in his den, where he told me his daughter was in her room. He encouraged me to go in and talk to her, and I did. Once in the room, I noticed the girl was heavy and appeared at least 17 years old. She was wearing a house coat. When I asked her what happened, she looked at me and replied, "They fucked me."

I immediately told her to get dressed and go with her parents, whom I had instructed to follow me to Pitt Memorial Hospital in Greenville. Once there, she was examined by a doctor who came to me and said, "Yes, she has had sex, but it wasn't the first time."

Walking into her room, I asked her, with the doctor present, if she had had sex before. She said, "Yes, I like it." Then she told me who was present, where they were, and that she had consented with all five boys.

When I arrived at Snow Hill at about 7 AM the following day, I called the District Attorney, Donald Jacobs, at his home. When I told him the quality of the case, which I thought it was, I asked if we should charge the boys. Jacobs told me we did not have a case because even though the girl was only 14, she looked 17. She had encouraged the sex, saying she liked it. She had gone to the location with the boys for sex, having known them, and agreed with the sex. Each boy may have known her, or they may have thought she was older than 14. I never found that out. Jacobs ended the investigation when I told him of her willingness for sex. Like I said, she did not look 14.

I called the father and told him of the DA's decision, and for weeks, the father would follow the five boys and shoot at them as they entered bars in Greenville. Several times, he was charged with attempted murder after shooting at them. However, the man never hit any of the five boys. Later, I was notified that the father was missing and had not been located.

I was riding one night with a friend from Greenville who went to college with me. As we turned onto the street near my residence, a guy from Walstonburg ran out and called my name. My friend was driving his Datsun 240Z, and we had the windows down. As was customary, I had my service pistol in my lap, a Smith and Wesson .357 magnum. The person calling my name was loud and boisterous. I would have expected no less from him, having known him for some time. His name is unimportant because he died many years ago. Suddenly, he looked down and saw the pistol in my lap.

"What will you do with that pistol?" he asked. "I'm going to blow your brains out if you fuck with me," I said, and with that, he just backed away, and we drove off.

After finishing Highway Patrol School and being assigned in Gates County, Bill Thompson, with the SBI, called to tell me he had located the merchant's body beside an open turkey range near Hookerton, North Carolina. The merchant was the father of the 14-year-old that was raped by five boys and had gone missing.

Bill called me regularly. I recall him telling me when Johnny Boykin was paroled in Walstonburg. Bill reminded me that Boykin had threatened to kill me and told me to be careful.

According to Bill, the merchant had accompanied another man to the herring nets in Hookerton. As they went in, there was a man hunting squirrels. When they left, they again passed the man hunting. This time, the man hunting shot the merchant as he turned away from him after speaking. When he fell, he looked at his friend who was with him and asked for help. The friend replied, "I'll help you, you son of a bitch" and shot the merchant in the head, killing him.

Bill's investigation revealed that both the wife and daughter had paid these two men to kill the merchant. The ironic thing was that they paid them only about $500 altogether. When the body was found, there was about $2,000.00 in his wallet. There was no evidence of any of those boys being involved.

One of my most extensive investigations involved a man named Johnny Boykin. After I went to work in the Sheriff's office, the Sheriff stationed me in Walstonburg, in the northern part of the county.

Throughout my time in Walstonburg, I received information about the involvement of Johnny Boykin in criminal activity involving stolen cars and any criminality, even murder.

I investigated stolen pigs and forgery, robbery and murders, suicide and rapes, but this one case was my most significant case, and I worked it the hardest.

On one occasion, I was told of a vehicle stolen from Virginia Beach and taken to Boykin's home and shop. The Chief Deputy and a Division of Motor Vehicles Inspector went to his home shop the next day. There was nothing there to show that the car had ever been there. It had been stripped down, sold, and removed from the location.

Before I left to go to Patrol School, I investigated a case where a young man broke into his brother's home and stole some guns. My investigation was conducted based on information from the brother's friends, who were also his accomplices. They told me that they had sold the weapon to Boykin for $60 and a pound of marijuana. Eventually, all three, including the victim's brother, told me the same story. Each of them pleaded guilty with the condition of a lesser sentence if they testified against Boykin, who had bought the guns.

I had met the young men who testified before when an informant told me this guy had some drugs in his bathroom. I went and looked, but honestly, I found nothing. After leaving the bathroom briefly, I returned to the bathroom and found a single bag of pot hidden in a towel. That was before the simple possession law was passed, which made less than an ounce, only a $100 fine, and when He could have received six months in prison, but of course, he didn't. I was looking with a warrant and did not leave the area, so the warrant was still valid.

Several times, Johnny Boykin's wife, Faye, called me in the middle of the night and told me she would die at his hands because he would kill her. I can't say if that was the reason, but I understand Johnny Boykin had a new girlfriend, who later became his wife. He would ride by her home, and he would shoot at her. This came to fruition when, one night, she was found in Pitt County dead under an overturned car. When I called the Trooper who investigated the accident in Pitt County, I told him of her fears; he replied, "She was drunk." I told him she didn't drink, and he replied, "She did this time." I don't know why the Trooper ignored my plea for further investigation, but he sure did.

I eventually was able to charge Boykin with receiving stolen weapons, and the three boys who stole the guns testified against him.

My investigation heated up when Boykin failed to appear in court. Just five minutes before court was scheduled to begin in Greene County, he checked into a hospital in the State of Virginia. I drew up a warrant and found him, with the help of informants, hiding behind a rotten mattress in Wilson County. Two deputy sheriffs from Wilson County met me, and I told them I knew where Johnny was and showed them the warrant. The Deputy Sheriff helped me locate him. I cuffed him and took him to jail. He told me, "Just take these cuffs off, and I'll whip your ass." I replied, "I've already won Johnny, you're in cuffs." Finally, he came to court, and his attorney asked for a continuance.

Don Jacobs, the District Attorney for the 8th Judicial District, told the judge, "You may want to read this, your honor, before making that decision." The statement was a transcript of a taped conversation in which the father of one of the people already convicted of stealing the guns and selling them to Boykin spoke to Boykin. The father was aware he was being taped. Boykin gave him $250.00 in cash and a check for $250.00 dated the day court was supposed to be over and told the father to tell his son, who was serving time for stealing the guns from his brother, that all he had to do was say to the court he couldn't remember what happened. He told the father that a Highway Patrolman couldn't remember what he said from one day to the next, and this boy couldn't either. Of course, he didn't know we were taping his conversation, but the daddy did.

Before the court, I was called to a break-in beside Boykin's

44

house. The owner was gone for the weekend. Riding with me that night was a volunteer fireman from Walstonburg who lived near the house. The fireman knew they were gone as he lived across the road.

When I pulled up in the yard, I had cut off my lights and the blue lights. I rolled into the yard and got out, handed the fireman a shotgun, and told him to stand in the front yard and fire it at them if anyone came out the front door. I then went to the back door, standing open, and listened. I heard three different voices. I yelled, "Police, you are surrounded."

I listened and LISTENED as the three criminals became frantic. One yelled, "There's a guy with a shotgun outside! They entered the back room one by one, got down on the floor, and lay with their hands behind their heads.

I called the fireman, and he came running. I told him to put his gun on the other two and, if they flinched, shoot them. At this point, he was positioned like a soldier at a shooting contest, bringing the gun to his head and shoulder. I handcuffed each one and called for backup, and when a couple more deputies arrived, I went to Snow Hill to process the three men. They were all tried in the following months and found guilty of Breaking and Entering and Attempted Larceny. They immediately appealed. Before I left Greene County, all of their appeals had been rejected, and they had been sentenced to prison.

Now, cutting back to the other trial:

When Johnny Boykin was brought before Judge Richard Alsbrook of Roanoke Rapids, the judge looked at the sheriff and told him to lock him up, saying, "We would try him on Thursday."

I then told the Judge, "I like your style. How long have you been on the bench, Judge?" Alsbrook looked at his watch and said, "30 minutes." He had just been appointed to the Superior Court by the Governor. He acted more like someone with a lengthy resume on the Superior Court Bench than a new Judge. Because of Boykin's efforts to avoid trial, Judge Alsbrook ordered him detained to ensure he would be present for court.

Boykin was eventually tried and sentenced to 7 years in prison and, after just a few months in prison, was pardoned by the Governor who had appointed the judge, James B. Hunt. Of course, I was told Boykin had some heavy hitters or people with deep pockets of cash in Greene County who petitioned the Governor for a pardon, and because of politics, that is what it usually takes.

Shortly after that, he was arrested in Moore County, where he jumped from a truckload of stolen tobacco and fell on a plow, knocking his teeth out. He was again sent to prison for the larceny of the tobacco. I'm unsure how much time he received from this charge or what he served.

Many years later, my wife and I were eating at Wilbers Restaurant when Boykin came in. Although he had made many threats to my life, I told my wife who he was. She asked, "Do we need to leave?" I told her, "He didn't recognize me, so why leave?" And he didn't.

I know I told you about how Donald Ray Shivar was violent, but I should have told you I was, too. I didn't think about it then. It was so long ago, but thinking back, my violence is becoming more apparent to me. Yet, I do not think I could have survived without occasionally displaying my form of violence, which was not meant as violence but rather meant to keep me alive—a kind of survival instinct.

Usually, I would run around Walstonburg to stay in shape. My friend from ECU would come over, and we had measured off a three-mile section in town to run in.

One afternoon, we were running when a car came by and threw a beer bottle at us. It was our practice to run with a 25-cal—automatic pistol in our hands. I had aimed the 25-cal. at the car and pulled the trigger. About the time I fired it, my friend slapped my hand, and the bullet went up in the sky. Of course, after I realized what could have happened had I hit anyone in that car, I was glad my hand was slapped. More importantly, I was glad nobody was hit. Still, I was mad with the occupants of the car, whom I recognized. I told my friend I would get them for throwing that beer bottle at me.

Later that night, when I came into town from work, at about 3 AM, I saw the car sitting unattended under the gas station awning at the corner of the street. I looked, but no one was around it or in sight. So, I returned to my rented room and changed out of my uniform. I went into the kitchen, and the lady I rented the room from had an unopened two-pound bag of sugar on the table. I took the sugar, placed a $5 bill in its place, and walked to the car. Still, no one was around or in sight. So, I opened the gas tank, poured the bag's contents into the tank, walked back home, and went to bed.

I never saw the car or the guys that drove it again, but I'm sure they know who ruined their car.

Today, yes, I'm sorry that thing happened that way. If I had shot them, I would have been in prison, and the way I did it just ruined a car. I had to get the message to them that I was not going to be hit with a beer bottle or anything else and do nothing about it. They and their friends had to learn that Bronnie Quinn was no one to be rude to. I meant that then as I do now. I tried not to disrespect people and would not accept it myself.

One of the cases I found easy to work on was forgeries. I'd get the person suspected of the fraud to give me a handwriting sample and send the sample and the forged note, usually a check, to the State Bureau of Investigation lab for analysis. In about a month, I had the person charged, and if the evidence was good enough, it was usually a conviction.

Some nights, we would get information about a hog theft and lay on the ground around the hog farms, hoping to catch the person who planned to steal the hogs. I would lie securely on the ground to see the culprit. Usually, nothing happened. Later in my career, I found it was because the stealing workers knew we were there and didn't steal anything that night. Later, when I became a

Private Investigator, most of these cases involved someone working for the owner. The owner was gone that weekend, so the worker would just report the hog dead but kill them himself and claim it was an honest death while selling the hog for substantial cash, usually $100 per hog, depending on the size. The Milling Company would allow so many honest deaths without penalty to the grower. So, you can see how stealing hogs could be a profitable job.

Serving warrants was a heavy task for a deputy. We all had warrants in the particular area in which we lived. One day, I spotted a guy for whom I had a warrant and stopped him. He had his baby with him and asked me to take the child to his parent's home so he could leave him with them. I stopped at his dad's side door, and he leaped out of the car and ran into the house with the child, dropping the child on the floor and out the front door. I went in after him, and he ran out the front door into a corn patch and was gone.

It took a few weeks, but I found out he would be at a local store through information from an informant. Since my wife was working at 264 Fish Fry Restaurant, I got her car and left my Sheriff's car there. I waited beside the store's building inside her vehicle. About five o'clock, I saw him walking down the side of the building in front of me. I was wearing a red coat over my sheriff's uniform, and he never suspected anything until I hit him and knocked him against the store. Apparently, he was looking down or did not recognize me until I leaped from the car, and then it was too late. I threw him against the car and handcuffed him, taking him first to the restaurant to change cars and then to jail.

One night after I was married, an older senior Deputy convinced the Sheriff that someone was threatening a local lady and that we should hide out at her home while her husband was away to try to catch him. He put another young deputy and me in the yard, watching for anyone coming into the house while he waited inside with the wife.

After about three hours, I realized we were his cover/ protection, and started complaining about the situation on the radio. He exited the house and figured the Sheriff would hurry and send us home. I just knew he was having an affair with the man's wife. Shortly after that, the man and his wife separated, apparently over such behavior. Don't get me wrong. While I disagreed with this kind of affair, I also didn't like him keeping me away from my wife to protect his interests.

Safety concerns got worse after my marriage. Death threats started coming more often. We lived in a mobile home that was more like a can than a home, but honestly, it was the best we could do. Things got so bad that I told Sherry, my wife, that if she heard shots, just dive to the floor and never start the car without checking it first for bombs. I even bought her a small pistol our first Christmas and taught her how to use it.

When I was working on the case of Johnny Boykin, he threatened me repeatedly.

At about that time, the movie Walking Tall came out. It tells the story of a sheriff in Tennessee who was killed for doing his job. While I had always been careful, I increased my diligence even more to be cautious.

One night, not long before leaving Greene County, I was on patrol near Maury when I found four Hispanics passed out, parked on the roadway with their car motors running. It was late at night, with little traffic, but the car was still in a curve. I walked up to the car and realized that all four men were unconscious. So, I just reached in and took them out one at a time and placed them handcuffed and bound in my car. I then pulled their car to the shoulder and transported them to the county jail. This just reminded me of the danger around every corner when driving. Often, it's not the danger you can see but the ones we can't see that are most deadly. Many times, I have gone around that very curve at a high rate of speed, and if the car had been there, then I would have killed them, and I would have died also.

A joint in Greene County outside Walstonburg was run by a small black man named Smokey. The cars would park on both sides of the road, and since traffic was light, I never had trouble there, and I never said anything. Occasionally, I would stop and park my car on the roadway with the blue lights on. I'd get out, lock my doors, and enter the bar. Smokey was a little man who wore a pistol on his side, one of those long-legged guns with a barrel that hung low. I never had trouble with Smokey or his joint, so I never spent much time there. Besides, he was always so courteous when I went in. There are places like Smokey's all over the world. Of course, they must be patrolled and shown that the law is always nearby whether or not they see us.

One day, I was called to a robbery on NC 903 near Scuffleton and Ormondsville. If memory serves me right, the little store was run by Mr. Tommy Bowen. You would know the store today because even though it's closed, there is a round Pepsi sign on the side of the building that says PEPSI 5 CENTS. Again, Mr. Bowen was the owner-operator, and someone had come in, robbed him, and beat him almost to death. When I arrived, Early Whaley was already there. Before the rescue carried him off, Mr. Bowen told Whaley who the robber was. Whaley and some of the other deputies went to locate the man, but when they found him, he was hunting with a group, who told Whaley he had been with them all day.

Mr. Bowen died that night of injuries he received from that beating without the robber, now murderer, ever being found. Even a reward could not help in finding the culprit. People sometimes do bad things, and even more often than not, they get away with it, but that doesn't stop the Police from trying to gather all the evidence. Who knows, maybe one day, this case will appear as an unsolved case, and the evidence I gathered will convict the person who murdered Mr. Bowen.

One night in 1975, I was dating a girl from the Bullhead section of Greene County, and when we were returning to her home from that date.

About a quarter mile from her home, I saw a car flipped over in the field. I immediately stopped and ran to where the driver was lying. The car was upside down, and the driver was lying beside the car door on the right side of the inverted car. I told my date to take my car and call the rescue, and I ran to the man on the ground.

Upon arriving at the driver, I noticed his right leg was inverted backward, opposite his usual stance. I scooped his head up in my arms, and at that moment, he took a breath and died.

I met and married my wife and transferred to the Sheriff's Department then. On my first date with Sherry, I went on a raid while she went to the restaurant to work until she returned to the courthouse and picked me up. She quickly learned my commitment to my job, and I discovered her commitment to our relationship. I kept her, and we were married in October, about a year and a half later.

Just before I got married, I received information about two boys in the Cobbs Crossroads area who were selling drugs. I was told that the person had seen the drugs in their home, a tiny 12x50 ft. mobile home. I quickly got a search warrant, went to the trailer, and found the two boys at home. I searched the trailer and found the drugs. In those days, marijuana was considered by older people to be a terrible thing. As I exited after finding the drugs, the owner of the trailer, Mr. Floyd Strickland, asked me what I had seen. The boys stood there, and I walked over to them and told them I had found the pot. When Mr. Strickland heard me say that, he looked at the two young men and said, "Get out now."

Almost immediately, I remembered Johnny Watkin's. Since I needed a place to live, I went to the side with him and asked if I could rent the trailer, and he replied, "Certainly." I moved in until we were married, and then Sherry moved in.

We were married in October and remained in the trailer until March when I went to Highway Patrol school. Then, Sherry moved in with her parents, and I stayed there on weekends, too.

TRIAL & ERROR

Everything was good for us newlyweds, except for the threats I would get back then. Occasionally, Trooper, my white German shepherd dog, would get off his leash and chase and kill my neighbors' cats. They understood, and maybe they were secretly glad the cats were gone because they never made a big deal out of it.

My home was right down the road from Wesley and Gladys Oakley. We visited and, once again, became dear friends, as we had always been. One day, Sherry was driving to Wilson, going a little too fast, and struck a ditch. I was hard on her because I feared Wesley would give her a ticket. That fear soon faded when Wesley told me to get off her back. Not only was he not going to charge her, but he was taking her side about going too fast.

I soon learned that my landlord, Mr. Floyd, was a Jehovah's Witness. While I could speak to him any day except Saturday, that day was off-limits. He wouldn't come to the door or talk to you about anything that day. Any other time was fine, but he was a good landlord. He charged me about $80.00 a month and took care of anything I needed to have done.

I recently found a light bill I got when I lived in that tiny trailer. It was only $30.00 for a whole month, and that was cheap. I only made $8600.00 a year, and with $80.00 in rent and food, I didn't have much money.

The night before I was married, my friend from college, David Brown, stayed with me because he was to be an usher at my wedding the next day. That night was cold. I had no skill in lighting heaters or anything else mechanical. Needless to say, the trailer was cold. While I attempted to light the pilot, I never could. It was only after I got back from my honeymoon that I got Mr. Floyd to light it for me. Mr. Floyd taught me his good nature and manners whenever he came over to help me.

Chapter Five: 63rd Basic Highway Patrol School

Being allowed into the 63 Basic Highway Patrol school was the most tremendous honor I ever received, but I was not yet a member of the State Patrol. I had to pass the 16-week course, and there was typically a 20% washout rate. I was amazed that I was there since I was the son of a construction worker who had never made more than $25 or $30.000 a year. My parents were not well educated, but I was still allowed in such a prestigious organization. I felt honored to be there and suspected many had a far better background than me.

I remember leaving that day for the class. I got up and went to the barber to get a haircut, but when I arrived, we were all standing outside the building in the parking lot when Trooper R.L. Peterson came out. I had heard of him and was amazed just to be there. Then the surprise set in. No one gave me anything. I had to earn it and earn it; I did for 16 weeks. I was a slave, and for the next 26 years, the Highway Patrol could tell me what to do and think. I could do nothing if I didn't want to face obstacles.

"You want to be Troopers," he yelled. "Get your ass over there in a line. What the hell are you doing on my grass? Why are you walking? Run. Run. Run." From then on, for the next 16 weeks, it was run everywhere you went. No walking, yes sir, no Sir. Then we went to the barbershop, and I got a haircut again. Again, I had to pay for it too.

We got in bed at about 11 o'clock the first night, and Peterson kicked in the door at 4:30 a.m. "Get the hell up out of that bed. Fall out now."

There were pushups, jumping jacks, and squats, and then we ran and ran and ran. I thought I was in shape but soon discovered I wasn't.

Then Trooper Frank Birch took over, and we ran some

more. Birch ran so fast one day that he almost caught a rabbit ahead of us.

I was ready to go home—but I couldn't. I had left a great job with the sheriff, but now I didn't think I could return. I had a new wife, so I had to stay. One guy left so fast that he left money in his drawer at school, and the Lieutenant ran after him. He missed him, and the cadet got away and lost his money.

For 16 weeks, there were geography, economics, law, and etiquette classes, as well as physical training.

The 10th week was defensive tactics. From physical training to fire watch, someone was assigned to watch for fires and burglaries for two hours every night. Week ten was particularly ominous.

When we got to Fire Watch, you were given a pitcher of alcohol and a bag of mouthguards, which were usually covered in blood. Your job while you stood watch was to wash the mouthguards in the alcohol. We all knew they were there for us the next day when we boxed.

Boxing was when two boxers entered a ring made by the cadets on the green grass behind the barracks. After the boxing, the green grass was replaced with red blood on the ground.

When I finally arrived home at the end of the ten weeks, I begged Sherry, my wife, "Please don't touch me; I hurt so bad." We had defensive tactics that week.

There was driving, defensive driving, and pursuit, which took time. We even took the bus to the racetrack at Maxton, an old Air Base, where we practiced and practiced driving. In the end, we graduated. I had been given my supply of uniforms, my guns, and my car.

While I had graduated, that still did not mean I was a trooper. While my title was Trooper, I still had six weeks of field training from my Field Training Officer, who could decide not to approve me. I was a Trooper by name only. No one let me forget that, from the time we left the school until the day I retired. I was on a leash and often worked under a gun, never knowing if my supervisor was hurting my career or not.

At any rate, I graduated from the 63rd Basic School in June 1978 and was assigned to Gates County in the Northeastern part of the state. I graduated 30 out of 63 cadets.

Chapter Six: Gates County Trooper

Gates County had the most significant US Coastguard base just east of it in Elizabeth City and a fantastic shoreline on the Chowan River. While Gates County in 1979 was essentially primitive, vast improvement in growing and creating new residents was possible. An increase in population would likely increase the business community and the income of many people in Gates County.

I expected Gates County to be similar to Greene County, but it was pretty different. Gates County seemed to be 30 years behind the rest of the world in terms of its thinking and behavior.

This is not to say there were not good people there, because there were, but the whole county functioned more like living in a 1940s county than a county in 1978. For instance, on Wednesday, the stores and banks closed at noon. There were only three restaurants in the whole county. The population was 8,000 people. Most were either pulp woods workers or worked in one of the shipyards in Virginia. There were two restaurants, bar be-que houses on opposite sides of the county, and a grade C sanitation place in Gatesville. The Grade C was good food. However, the place had been an old walk-in theater soda shop. The man who owned it would not fix it up, so you might be eating fried chicken and see a roach walking down the wall.

To make matters worse, the person who ran it needed to be endowed with more personality. She was about 85 years old and did not tolerate people well. For example, a young man walked in and said, "When you get time." Before he could say anything else, she said, "That's right. Sit down and shut up. I'll get to you."

Gates County was more in tune with Southern Virginia than Northeastern North Carolina. Television and radio stations came from Virginia, and getting a North Carolina station was difficult. In addition, the Gates County Sheriff's radio was in sync with the Suffolk, Virginia Ultra High frequency and not close to any radio frequency in North Carolina. Gates County had no jail, just a holding cell. Prisoners were taken to Hertford County, but after the county got a deputy, that changed, and prisoners were taken by the sheriff, who had only one deputy, to Chowan County, 30 miles away. You can see how this might create a problem for the sheriff and the troopers.

The courthouse parking lot's lights were on the opposite side of the building from where troopers parked with prisoners. Sometimes, they would be lost in the darkness when you exited your car with a prisoner. It was only luck that they didn't just run or hurt us.

One night, I had not handcuffed the prisoner and parked in the rear of the building. When I exited the car, I lost sight of the prisoner, but lucky for me, I went to the courthouse door where the light was, and he followed me to the light.

I realized he could have hurt me or gotten away, so the next week, I went to the Commissioners to beg for a light and explained why I needed it. They assured me a light would be put in, but when it was placed in operation, it was on the north side of the building, entirely on the other side from where I would go to my office.

By May 5th, 1979, Pete Peterson was dead and buried in Black Mountain, North Carolina. I remember Pete coming to our rooms the last night we were in school before graduation, and he said to me, "Quinn, you are going to Gates County." "Yes, sir," I said. "You will be the only one there, so be careful." "Yes, sir, Trooper Peterson, sir, you didn't think I would graduate, did you?" I said. He smiled and said, "Quinn, I had no doubts about you graduating." When I got to Gates County, I placed a picture of Pete and an earlier school running with a sign that said fifty-five reasons to drive fifty-five. Of course, 55 cadets were running in the picture.

Pete had been working in Rutherford County and got a

call about a man who had shot and killed two Rutherford County Deputies, one being the high sheriff's brother.

The two deputies had gone to the man's home concerning a complaint they had gotten about his daughter, who had graduated from the local high school. She had put alcohol in the punch at an after-graduation party.

The man became irate and threatened his daughter. When the deputies arrived, he just shot them down in the drive, killing both deputies. He fled the scene, and Pete clocked him at a high speed and turned around to pursue him.

When Pete rounded the curve, the man was out of his car and shot him with a 30-06 rifle, striking Pete between the eyes and killing him instantly. The man, who had also killed someone else while in the military, walked around the car, shooting out all four tires before going into the woods.

All night, he talked to officers from the woods where he was hiding as they looked for him. When he was told that no one was dead, he said: "I know better than that; that trooper is dead; I saw him."

Finally, at about daybreak, he surrendered and was taken into custody. After a trial, He was sentenced to death and eventually was put to death in the state's gas chamber.

I remember going to the office in Ahoskie on May 1, 1979, where Barbara Warren, the Troop C District 2 Secretary, told me about the shooting. Each troop and district has a secretary to assist in managing reports and customer service. To me, Pete Peterson was a God, and no one man could kill him. Pete was a black belt in Karate and knew how to defend himself, but it was true. He was dead.

I left for a local gas station to get a copy of the Raleigh News and Observer's story version. It was true.

I went back to Gates County and met Sherry in Gatesville, where I told her about the shooting and just sat on the curbing and cried like a baby.

I said I fought hard in the Sheriff's office, but the Highway

Patrol was worse. I was the only trooper working the entire county, which meant 350 square miles. When I went to Gates County, there was only one sheriff with no deputies. Even when he did get a deputy, it was just one, and he was usually in bed when I was working.

I remember the week before my oldest son was born, I stopped a crane operator from Portsmouth, Virginia. I placed him under arrest, but that was when we didn't handcuff anyone unless they gave us trouble.

Once I got to the breathalyzer room, he turned his back on me and put his hand in his pants. I told him not to do that, and suddenly, he did it again. I popped his head with my convoy. A convoy is a piece of metal on a spring wrapped in leather. He calmed down and sat down, but he was up doing the same thing again in a few minutes.

I went to strike him, and he fell on top of me in the corner of the building. I had his long shoulder-length hair in my left hand wrapped around the three middle fingers and pulled him closer to me so he couldn't get any leverage on his swings. He hit me, and I returned each of his blows with my convoy, which threw blood from his head all over the ceiling.

I called Frank Rice, the magistrate on duty whose office was across the hall, and he came running into the room. Frank was a very feminine person who was a great person but not made for fighting. He kicked the man in the back, which only made him madder. So, I told him to go to the car and get my baton.

Frank ran out the door, and a few seconds later, he came back inside and hit the guy with my baton, but that didn't faze him either.

I felt myself fading. So, I raised him with my knees and kicked him in the testicles, and he went flying across the room. When he came back toward me, I pulled my .357 magnum pistol and aimed it between his eyes. Finally, he stopped and backed up. Frank and I left the room, locking him inside. As we looked in through the outside windows, we could see him as we called for help on the car radio, standing in the rain. The man was going around the room looking for something, anything, to wipe away the blood on his head.

I called for help, and as I did, I heard every car in Hertford County check out for dinner as I stood in the rain and waited. I watched this guy take Trooper Sam Armstead's reports and wipe away the blood from his scalp. Armstead was off and had left his reports on the desk for me to take to Ahoskie when I turned in mine.

About 20 minutes passed, and Deputy Ronnie Stalling from Hertford County arrived to help. I told him to wait as we had locked the man in the courthouse. I already knew that patrol personnel were en route.

Another 30 minutes passed, and suddenly, Sergeant Herb Conway of the Highway Patrol arrived, and we went in. Conway looked at the man and asked him, "What in the hell were you doing?" He replied, "I just didn't want him to hit me anymore."

Conway ran the breathalyzer, and we carried him before Frank for the bond hearing. Suddenly, he leaned his head over, and a glob of blood fell on the floor. I thought Frank was going to pass out. Frank screamed, "Oh my God, I've killed him," to which I replied, "What do you think he was trying to do to us?"

He was processed, and with his bond set, I carried him to the emergency room in Ahoskie. There, the doctors said he needed 15 stitches in his head. He got the stitches, and then I carried him to the jail in Winton and turned him over to a jailer.

I was sore when I arrived home at about 5 am, and my pregnant wife saw me in the tub soaking. My uniforms were all soaked in blood and lay in a pile on the floor. I thought she was going to have our son right there, but she waited for another week before giving birth. Luckily, her parents were there that weekend to help me with her.

A few months later, my then-brother-in-law was visiting

me from Jones County. I asked him if he wanted to go riding with me. I'm sure I got permission from my Line Sergeant first, but I can't remember. I stopped a car right down the road from a beer joint outside Murfreesboro and found a rifle visible from outside the vehicle under the driver's seat. I placed the man in the patrol car, but as I returned to the car, my brother-in-law saw a group of people leaving the joint and running towards us. When I got to the patrol car, he had locked the doors and would not open them. Luckily, I had a key in my pocket, and I retrieved the rifle, unlocked the door, and got in before pulling off. We discussed my safety. I never let him ride with me again. I tried to explain to him the danger he put me in.

While driving home for lunch one Sunday, I met a guy I knew well who was going in the opposite direction. His name was Milton Ulysses Leech, and I knew his license had been revoked. I turned around. As I approached his car, he pulled into a driveway. He jumped out and ran to the passenger side as his girlfriend Barbara slid into the driver's seat.

I told Him, "Milton, you are under arrest for driving while your driver's license has been revoked." Milton replied, "Na, Na, Na Quinn, damn if we don't fight," to which I took off my glasses and my hat and laid them on my patrol car and told Milton, "Let's do it; I'm late for dinner." Milton just looked at me and said, "Where do you want me to sit, Quinn?" I cuffed him and put him in the car, and we went to the magistrate's office. Before the court, Milton was stabbed in a poker game and killed, so that ended that.

On another night, I was about to go home when, at 11:30 pm, I received a call about a collision on US 13 at the state line.

When I arrived, a man stood beside the car in the ditch. The back seat was where the driver's seat was supposed to be. I asked him if this was his car and if he was the driver. He replied, "No, he's at my house trying to get in." I asked him why he wasn't up there. I jumped in my car and drove the 500 feet to his back door. There, I found a man beating on the door. Looking out the window was a woman and two children with eyes as big as Mason Jar's lids.

I came up behind him, tapped him on the shoulder, and said, "I'm Trooper Quinn, and I'm here to investigate your wreck," to which he replied, "I'm not going no fucking where."

Again, I tapped him and said, "I'm Trooper Quinn, and I don't care if you go laying on a stretcher or standing up, but you are going."

He stopped, looked at me, and said, "Who did you say you were?" Again, I said, "My name is Quinn, and I'm here to investigate this wreck," to which he said, "Where do I sit?" and started walking down the steps.

I investigated the accident and arrested him for driving impaired. When the wrecker came, we went to the courthouse in Gatesville. Shortly after we got there, he started complaining of feeling bad. I called the only doctor in the county who came out and examined him and told me he was just inebriated. Trooper Armstead, a black Trooper, ran a breathalyzer, and his reading was above the legal limit, so I carried him before Abraham Saunders, the magistrate, who set his bond. I released him to a black deputy for transport to the jail.

About a month went by, and a black lawyer called me to the courthouse and wanted to know why I had mistreated the man so badly. I asked, "How was he mistreated?" The lawyer said, His neck was broken." To that, I replied the following:

"A black doctor said he was inebriated, a black trooper said his blood alcohol was above the legal limit, a black magistrate set his bond, and a black deputy took him to jail; I'm just the white guy that arrested him."

I never heard anything further about this case.

Some nights, the magistrates were only on call. Those wanting a magistrate would have to open the door across the hall, go into their office, and call for them on the phone. Then I had to wait for them to arrive from their homes. This also created a problem because the prisoner could get up and run out of the building while we were gone, handcuffed or not. When I asked for a phone, I got it, but it was a party line with the magistrate's office, and I couldn't use it if anyone was on it and vice versa.

Of course, this was good compared to the old days when troopers had to take the prisoner to the magistrate's home for adjudication, traveling all over the county to the magistrate's homes.

At any rate, I learned and grew, and that was the point.

I worked in Gates, Bertie, and Hertford Counties, an area approximately 1400 square miles from the Roanoke River to the Virginia line, sometimes alone.

Of Course, Bertie and Hertford were different. They had their jails and more deputies and worked on North Carolina frequencies. You could see North Carolina TV, so you got NC News in these two counties.

Gates County and the whole area was about 60% black and 40% white. I found that I had a better relationship with Blacks than Whites in Gates County. This was because of just three people, including Reverend Howard Mitchell, whom I was extremely close to. Howard and I became close friends early in my career in Gates County. I felt, he thought, a great deal of me. Not many days he and I didn't have breakfast together at his home. When he died, his wife called me and told me he had passed away. She asked if I would be a pallbearer, and I said yes. Even more important to me was that when my wife and I arrived at Mill Neck Church for the service, I was directed to my seat with the pallbearers while the funeral director took my wife to sit with the family.

Howard was my friend. He gave me good advice on how to talk to people, and I would listen to him intently. It always proved to be good advice.

Another Black man I listened to was Abraham Saunders, a

close friend and confidant. Abraham was a magistrate and was fair and just when I brought a person before him, no matter the color.

Abraham was also a leader in a black group in Gates County that would decide if a white had mistreated a black.

Abraham was so close to me that when I retired from the Highway Patrol, he and his son drove from Gates County to Goldsboro to attend my retirement party. Abraham was a true friend. When I told him I was running for US Marshal, but I didn't have help outside of North Carolina, he directed me to see certain blacks for their support.

One day, a black man came inside his office and said, according to Abraham, that this "Highway Patrolman Quinn was tough on black people." Abraham quickly replied, "Yes, he is, but he is tough on whites too, and that is what we want—fairness."

I arrived in Gates County with a chip on my shoulder. I had spent 16 weeks being yelled at, running, and cussed at, thinking I could fight a grizzly bear if I had to. Any reason to fight that bear became welcomed by me.

Our reports had to be turned in for the year by December 31, 1978. In January 1979, a guy came to my door, telling Sherry, "He needed me to investigate an accident he had on December 27th, 1978."

I was sick with the flu and was lying in bed when I heard my wife answer the door. I could listen to the conversation, and Sherry said, "I don't think he will investigate it, but I'll ask him." She came and got me and told me he wanted me to investigate a collision that occurred in December.

I was sick, and I felt like crap anyway. I walked the short distance from the bedroom of the mobile home where we stayed to the front door where the man was standing.

"What kind of wreck did you say you had?" I asked. "Well," I continued, "I can investigate that for you, but I'll have to give you a ticket for not reporting it by the quickest means of communication." To that, he yelled, "You can't do that," and it ticked me off. I was ticked off and sick. He came to me wanting me to investigate his collision later than he should. He was crazy.

"You're right," I said. "I can't do that, but I'll tell you what I can do. I'm going to my bedroom and get my gun, and if you're standing here when I get back, the undertaker is going to drag your body off my yard. Do You Hear ME?" I screamed. With that, I slammed the door, went to the bedroom, and got my gun. When I returned, his car was gone, and he was too.

Early in Gates County, I was called to a school bus collision. Abraham was there, and one of his five boys, Benjamin, was driving one of the buses. I explained to Abraham that I would have to charge Benjamin. Abraham said," Mr. Quinn, I have raised my boys as best I could, but you must understand their mama was there too."

That was Abraham's fairness and respect for the law.

One incident involved a man from New Jersey. Curley J. Hooper. I stopped him for speeding on US 158, and he accused me of pulling my gun on him. I didn't pull my gun, but I placed my elbow on the handle of the gun while talking to him. He filed a complaint against me with the state's Attorney General, the Governor, and the NAACP.

While driving through Ahoskie that day, I saw Howard at the Post Office and told him I had a problem. He immediately asked me what it was. I showed him the complaint, and he looked at me and said, "Mr. Quinn, I can handle the Governor, I can handle the State Attorney General, and I think I can handle the NAACP." I didn't hear anything else about the complaint but was acquitted.

One day after I first got to Gates County, Bill Eure, the Sheriff, called me and asked if I would help him with an accidental shooting in Eure. Two 12-year-olds were rabbit hunting, and one shot the other. The bullet struck the boy behind the ear, killing him instantly. Of course, he was Sheriff and in charge, but he seemed lost as to what to do. He seemed shocked to be there, and the death of the boy seemed to deter his ability to process what was happening. Being new to the county, I figured that maybe he was family, and that was causing a problem.

Anyway, there wasn't a lot to do because the boy who did the shooting told us what happened, and to be honest, I just thought how tragic it was.

The Sheriff hired a deputy a few years after I got to Gates County. This gave him a total of one. I was at the Roduco Store, and the deputy saw me. He was of average height and had significant facial hair. He had a beard unheard of for a deputy at that time. He was driving his unmarked car and wearing civilian clothes. I remember he told me that a man in the store for whom he had a warrant didn't believe he was a deputy and would not go with him.

Upon supplying me with proof of his identification, I went inside and told the man he was a Deputy Sheriff, and he better go because the next step, if he refused, would be for both of us to whop his ass. The man went with him.

Another person I was close to was Frank Rice. When I first went to Gates County, Frank filed a complaint with my sergeant, telling him he thought I was too hard on people.

I met with Frank and explained that since he thought I was too rough, I would bring people into his office, plead my case, and go back across the hall to my office. He would have to handle it if they got out of hand, and he replied, "You're doing fine."

We became great friends, and often, he loaned his keys to his beach cottage at Kitty Hawk to Sherry and me. He would come to my home, and I to his. We were friends until his death.

When I arrived in Gates County, there had not been a trooper assigned for at least a year. I had to fight constantly, and I chased cars about every week. Still, I made about 107 DWI arrests the first year I was there.

After Sam Armstead got to Gates County, we both appeared

in an article in the county paper. The article started this way: "Probably no person in Gates County has been cussed more than Bronnie Quinn. Traffic deaths were mounting, and DWI and Speeding arrests were declining before Quinn. When Quinn got to Gates County, the deaths continually declined, and the tickets increased. Then Sam Armstead came to Gates County, and things improved and increased again.

The writer said that while citizens were cussing Quinn and Armstead, they saved lives, and the numbers proved it. Of course, this is simply a complete interpretation, but the paper is here to confirm what was said.

One day, I was at the local gas station having my car washed when one of the local game wardens saw me. He came up wide open toward me with his older grey Plymouth, which resembled a vehicle Johnny Boykin operated in Walstonburg. Immediately, I pulled my gun from the holster in self-defense, but seeing who it was, I put the gun back inside the holster. The locals at the gas station saw it and immediately called in a complaint to the Ahoskie office, and I was investigated for it.

I explained my situation and that I had received a call from State Bureau of Investigation Agent Bill Thompson, who warned me to be careful, and I was. It worked because nothing happened, and I was cleared.

This was just more proof of my attention to preserving my life. The training I received from people like Melvin and my superiors on the Highway Patrol instilled a sense of self-preservation in me. My training had prevented me from acting recklessly and firing that gun.

After I passed VASCAR School, I would sit near a substation on US 13 and make my week. Making my week is slang for issuing enough tickets to keep the Sergeant off your back. Simply put, there is no reason a decent Trooper couldn't write ten tickets each week in addition to investigating their share of collisions, many of which deserved a citation.

One week, I stopped a white Buick Rivera traveling South.

The male driver was about 4 feet 9 inches tall and weighed approximately 175 pounds. He was wearing a Karate Gee and jeans. During our conversation, he told me he was an Army Lieutenant. His driver's license showed his name as Richard Flaherty. He told me he had pulled two tours in Vietnam and was returning to Fort Bragg.

My first thought was that this guy was lying, but he was polite and well-mannered and never gave me a reason to suspect anything except that he was who he said he was. I issued him a warning ticket to slow down. I remember thinking, whoever saw a 4 ft 9-inch soldier in the US Army?

Last May, while in Boca Raton, Florida, visiting my son, a friend there asked if I had read about this guy who was killed in Miami. His name was Richard Flaherty, and he was a Captain in the US Army. He had pulled three tours of duty in Vietnam and was DEA in Miami working undercover. He was killed by a hit-and-run driver from Boca Raton who was drunk. I looked at his picture and, to my amazement, the man I had stopped years before.

A Miami officer had become his friend, and he told him what he was doing just before he died. He was homeless by his own choice, but the officer found passports and cash hidden in his campsite. In Vietnam, he was called the giant killer because of his karate skills and his tunnel capabilities when he went down into the tunnels and killed VC. When he was young, he wanted to be in the Army but knew he would have a hard time due to his height. So, he became a blackbelt. Then I realized this little man probably could have killed me if he had wanted to. You never know who you are dealing with.

When people get a little alcohol in them, they go completely crazy, as one of my neighbors in Gates County proved. He was only about 21 years old. His dad was a union welder who built high rises in New York and New Jersey. When his dad would go away for work, he was sometimes gone for a month or more.

Junior would cut loose. One night, I was on a late call and received a call about an accident on US 158 East near the Great Dismal Swamp. When I arrived, I found my neighbor's son drunk, known as Cooter Brown. (We sometimes use this description to describe a very impaired driver.) When I finished the investigation, I placed him under arrest.

When we got to the courthouse, he called his momma to come down, and she came with our pastor. We all went to the same church.

He checked too high on the breathalyzer, and the magistrate set his bond. Before he could get his mom to post his bond, he started cursing her, the pastor, me, and the Magistrate. This, of course, led to the judge issuing an order of commitment. I told our pastor to take the mom home, and when he sobered up, she could go to Winton and get him. I put him in the holding cell, and he went crazy, calling his mom a whore and using language you never would hear, espccially in front of your pastor.

On the way to the jail, he looked at me and spoke, "I'm going to rape your wife, run over your children and burn down your house."

I just pulled off the road, snatched him up by the throat, and told him that 20 years from now, if something happens to my wife or kids, even if she leaves a pot of water on the stove and the house burns, you will be the first SOB I'm coming to see. I continued driving and delivered him to jail.

The next day, he walked to my house and wanted to talk to me. I told him to go outside, and I'd be there in a few minutes. He looked at me and said, "You won't let me in your house?"

"No," I said, "Now go outside." He went to my patrol car, and I unlocked the doors, and he got in.

He began, "I want to apologize for what I said." To which I answered, "No."

"You ain't gonna accept my apology?" he said.

"No," I said.

"Well, why not?" he asked.

"Son, you didn't say anything you didn't want to say. That alcohol just gave you the courage to say it. Now let me tell you something. From this day forward, if you come by my house, you better cross over and walk on the other side of the road. If you put your toenail inside my property line, I will shoot off your foot. Do you understand me?"

"Yes, sir."

From that day forward, as long as I was in Gates County, if he passed my house, he would cross over to the opposite side of the road, walk past my home, and then cross over to the side he was initially on. I never heard anything from his parents about his manners or his case.

Being a trooper is tough. There is the work, the money, and the criticism, but also the scheduling. I had only one weekend per month off, and we usually used that weekend to go home.

While visiting Wilson at my in-laws' house, my father-in-law bought himself a new television with a remote control. As he showed it to me with all the pride one can have about getting such a device, I looked him in the eyes and told him, "I wouldn't have it."

"What?" he said, "this is great. Look, you don't even have to get up to change channels. Look, it's great."

I said," I wouldn't have it."

"What, what's wrong with you, boy? This is great," he said.

I looked at him unconcernedly and said jokingly, "I'm not so sorry that I can't tell your daughter to get up and change the channel."

To that, he just said, "shucks."

I had a great relationship with my mother and father-in-law; little things like this made it even better. He treated me the same way many times, and I loved both him and my mother-in-law greatly.

In late 1987, the Gates County Sheriff, Ray Harrell, called

me to assist him in a murder investigation. His Deputy, John Ballard, was sick, and Ray needed help. I located the home and found it was the residence of a man who was known for assaulting his wife. He had beaten her multiple times, and each time, she would indict him. He would beat her some more after she went home. He would even go to her parent's home if she left him and picked her up, dragging her home by the hair on her head. If her family tried to stop it, he would beat them, too.

On this particular occasion, he came home drunk and went to sleep on the sofa. The wife went to her bedroom, got his shotgun, and placed it on his chest. She chickened out and carried the gun back to the bedroom and put it where she found it, in the corner of the room. She walked back to the living room where her husband lay sleeping, building up courage, and again, after 15 minutes, she returned. Again, she retrieved the shotgun and walked back to the den. Placing the gun on her husband's chest, but this time, she did not chicken out and blew a hole in his chest the size of a fifty-cent piece.

She notified the Sheriff, who called me. When I arrived, he had her write statements about what had happened. She was charged with murder, and when she went to trial, Senator Frank Balance of Warrenton defended her. The husband got all the attention as one-by-one witnesses told of how he had abused her and how he would beat her. In the end, the jury saw no reason to send her to prison for killing him, and she was found not guilty.

The first fatal accident I investigated in Gates County happened one day when I was off and came to work at 6 pm. The accident occurred at 5 pm at Holly Grove Market. The deceased, driving a motorcycle, was driving on wet pavement. When he went around the curve on NC32 at the market, he just laid it down. It appeared to be only road rash and some burns as his only injuries.

We had a guy named Peter Harrell, who could only drive for the rescue squad as he could not pass the EMT certification. That day, as I finished the accident, when he returned to the scene, I asked, "How is he, Peter?" as he drove up with the rescue squad.

He looked at me and said, "Quinn, you know he died before we got to the State Line."

With that, his wife walked up and asked, "How is he?" and without even thinking, I said, "You know, he died before he got to the state line." I was insensitive and failed to consider how I responded to her. I was embarrassed for my actions and suspected that I would receive a complaint but never did, which did not relieve the shame of my actions, even today.

Two brothers, who were just terrors, lived in Corapeake. Back then, I would get tag repos if a registration tag had not expired, but the insurance on the vehicle had. I would go to the house to get the tag. These two brothers would play basketball outside. Knowing they would see me when I pulled up, they completely ignored me until I blew the horn. Then they had one of the brothers walk over to me and tell me the tags were in Virginia. I told them, "I'll be back one week from today, and you need to have the license here."

A week later, when I returned, they played basketball, but again, they ignored me; I would blow the horn. The same guy would come over. He told me he had yet to go to Virginia to get the tags. Now, mind you, the house was about ½ mile from the Virginia line, so I wrote him a ticket for not surrendering the tags.

About a month passed, and I was again in Corapeake when I saw his older brother driving a small 1972 Chevrolet Nova Car. I activated my blue light without really any reason to stop him, and when he pulled over to the shoulder and started to exit, I saw a car coming up behind me.so I remained in the patrol car. The older brother threw his car door open into the roadway just as the younger brother came by and took off his door. Seeing this was so funny that I cut my blue lights off, laughed, and drove away.

Two years after getting to Gates County, we bought our

first home. It had been the Baptist Parsonage in Hobbsville, on the east side of Gates County. My sister, her newborn daughter, and my 80-year-old grandmother came to help us move. When we began to move in, it began to snow. It continued the next day. I had sent Sherry to the town of Hertford in Perquimans County to buy a stove. The current power was off when she returned due to snowfall. We had no stove because it was electric, and we sat on the truck bed covered in snow.

When the snow stopped, it was almost up to the bottom of the windows. Grandma and my sister were snowed in at our house for over a week. When she did get to leave, she swore to me that she would never come back in the winter. She only did it once the temperature was at least 70 degrees. That Saturday night, when I went to work, I remember the snow coming down and getting so high that we had to follow graders from the DOT to get around. At about 10 PM, we were called on the radio and told to go home. That was the only time in my career that ever happened. When I got near my home, I was dispatched to an accident. It involved a drunk driver hitting a volunteer rescue squad vehicle. I finally arrived home at about 2 AM, but it was another cold night without heat.

I met my next-door neighbor Beatrice Hollowell that next day when she walked over in the snow and told us she had a gas stove and was cooking hot dogs. She asked if we would like to come over and eat, and of course, we did.

Beatrice became a second mother to both Sherry and me. We grew to love her with all our hearts. Sherry and I were off one weekend and planned to go to Wilson. That weekend, a neighbor called and told us Beatrice had passed away in her sleep. Sherry and I just held each other and cried uncontrollable tears for days after she left us.

One day before I left Gates County, Major James Langley, a dear friend who lived in Maury, called me on the radio and told me he was going to the Prison Unit in Gatesville. He asked if I would like to meet for lunch. I told him, "Sure," and he replied, "Be at the camp at noon."

Major Langley had been with the prison system for years, starting at seventeen. One day, he walked by Maury Prison, and the Superintendent asked him if he could work there. He said, "Yes."

"How old are you?" the Super asked.

Twenty-one," Langley said.

You want a job?"

"Yes," Langley said. The next day, he went to work for the North Carolina Prison system. Langley worked in the prison system, eventually rising to oversee security for eastern North Carolina. I met him in Maury once when he called and requested a deputy to help him with a matter related to his family cemetery plot.

Someone had knocked over his dad's tombstone and littered the cemetery with paper. I found out it was two local boys. Talking to them in the presence of their parents encouraged them to mow the cemetery, fix the tombstone, and pick up the paper, and Langley would probably be happy. It worked. Langley never forgot it. He often would call me to join him in Gates County at the prison when he was inspecting it.

When you go inside a prison, you become a prisoner. I locked my gun, my handcuffs, and my baton inside my trunk, along with my tear gas canister, and the guard on the gate would let me inside.

I walked about 50 yards toward the cafeteria and saw a tree running toward me. Of course, it wasn't a real tree, but the man was so big and tall that he resembled a tree. As he spoke, I had to look up at him to see his face.

"Do you remember me?" He yelled.

"You look familiar," I said.

"You put me here," he said.

"You having fun?" I asked him, walking around him fast.

I went straight to the cafeteria and told Major Langley about the encounter. He laughed at the incident, which made me aware of my situation. I remembered the man and when I had arrested him. He had a traffic collision on a rural paved road in Gates County and was quickly cuffed and placed inside the jail. He had about eight other charges for DWI pending, and at that time, DWI was worse than murder in the state system, so a conviction was easy back then. I saw some terrible accidents while in Gates County, and many were accidents that led to deaths. One accident came on a small, winding, two-lane road in western Gates County.

A 16-year-old's mother had bought him a new 240Z, and he was flying up a 45-mph maximum road with a 17-year-old boy and a 15-year-old girl in the car. The car ran off the right shoulder, striking an oak tree, crossing the roadway, striking another tree on the left before crossing back over and striking the third tree. At this point, the car flipped, throwing both the 17-year-old boy and the 15-year-old girl out, killing them instantly. The driver was thrown out, and the vehicle landed on top of him in the middle of the roadway and caught fire.

Two farmers were tending a field at that particular point and saw the car's collision and landing. They ran over and together pushed the vehicle off the young driver and saved his life, but then, law enforcement came into play.

At that time, in Gates County, the District Attorney wanted us to charge the worst charge, and if it was reduced, the defendant did the sentence. I charged the young 16-year-old with two manslaughter charges, which were later reduced to 2 deaths by vehicle charges. Manslaughter carried a possible 10-year prison sentence on each count.

There were often traffic accidents. There was a crash on January 10, 1993. I saw and worked the worst accident I have ever had to deal with.

Duane Banks was a trooper in training with his field training officer, Sam Armstead, who was assigned to an accident on US 13 North. When they got there, the road was covered in dead bodies, toys, and diapers. They called me to assist, and when I arrived, I wished they had not called me.

There were sheets over the body and body parts across the road, as well as diapers, toothpaste, and hot wheel cars.

A rescue squad member picked up a sheet to show me, and there was a leg stump. I remember seeing it and thinking it was a baby doll's leg, but then it hit me: it was a baby's leg. She then showed me the baby without a head, where it had stopped after it was decapitated.

Another 4-year-old was dragged down the highway, and his face had been removed.

The dad, a decompression expert from Camp Lejeune Marine base, and his family were going south on US 13 behind a large truck when the father attempted to pass with heavy rain coming down. He pulled out, and as he came to the point he could see, he hit a log truck traveling north head-on.

The father died instantly; the mother was seven months pregnant, and she died on the way to the hospital. She was holding a 4-year-old baby named Vincent, the only survivor, in her arms. His mom saw the truck and spun around, using her body to cushion the baby.

Things only worsened when a school bus full of kindergarteners unloaded. The driver walked them down to the scene to view the remains. I got mad about that, and later, I filed a complaint against the bus driver. The Superintendent told me about the local school system and that it was all right to do that. I assured him I had better never have that happen to my kids and left.

The largest, most extensive Coast Guard base in North Carolina is in Elizabeth City, just east of Gates County. In 1986, I was notified of a crash involving a small Cessna that crashed into a wooded area off a soybean patch near Buckland. I was told to watch for a Coast Guard helicopter hovering over the crash site at the back of the field,

I spotted the helicopter and crossed the soybeans to the edge of the woods. There, I jumped out and left my car sitting in the field.

About 200 yards inside the wood line, I found two Coast Guard airmen and four passengers injured. The airman was tending to one man with a wound over his nostrils, allowing the air to dissipate before he could breathe.

One Airman switched off and went to attend to the other wounded passengers while I attempted to give heart palpation compressions to the injured man the airman was working on. At that point, he began giving mouth-to-mouth while I continued to provide chest compressions. Frankly, the mouth-to-mouth and the chest compressions were not working, as with each attempt, I could see the air exiting the extra hole in his face.

Soon, a truck arrived, and the injured were placed in the truck and transported to the field. There, a helicopter landed so the passengers could be loaded and flown to the Elizabeth City hospital.

I knew this to be an excellent hospital, as I investigated many collision victims who wound up there. Unfortunately, the people of Gates County were not used to seeing a large helicopter up close. They flooded the bays to look inside. The pilots could not take off because of the danger the rotor posed. I remember that a helicopter on a Vic Morrow set crashed at about that same time, and Morrow was cut in half.

The airman and I were screaming for the people to back away from the helicopter, and after about ten minutes, we got their attention. Unfortunately, the man we were working on died either in flight or before they lifted off, although I never found out exactly when.

The next day, Trooper Keith Holland and I were checking driver's license on US 13 when a car pulled up, and the man driving asked if I was Trooper Quinn. I replied, I was, and he said, "Thank you for working on my dad yesterday. He died, but at least I know you tried."

Airplane crashes were constant occurrences in Gates County; I don't know why. Usually, the Sheriff had to wait all night until someone from the Federal Aviation Administration could inspect the plane after the crash. I'm glad we didn't have that responsibility.

US 158 was built right through the Great Dismal Swamp. It was built during an era when many roots and stumps were thrown into the road's foundation. Of course, the stumps, roots, and trees degraded and created sinkholes in the road, causing it to get very bumpy. This would lead to accidents because drivers were pulled across the center line and collided with oncoming vehicles.

On one occasion, I witnessed a tractor-trailer traveling to Elizabeth City bumping and bouncing so severely that the bottom of the trailer collapsed onto the roadway, spilling its contents.

During the worst cold spell I can remember, a similar thing happened on US 13 near Story on the western side of Gates County. A trailer hauling trees broke and dumped the trees on the roadway. It was freezing that day, and I had to stand outside the car and direct traffic while machines picked up the trees and put them on another trailer.

While working alone from 12 p.m. to 8 a.m. on another night in Gates, Hertford, and Bertie counties, I went to Winton to the Sheriff's office. As I went into Winton, I saw a brand-new Chrysler New Yorker traveling south out of Winton while I was going north toward the courthouse. I remember noticing that the Chrysler's trunk was raised open, which was unusual, but I did not have time to stop it. So I continued to the courthouse. After finishing my business, I traveled back to Gates County. As I neared Molley Perry's gas station, I came upon the same New Yorker ahead of me, and its trunk was still open.

I put the blue lights on, and the New Yorker pulled into Molley Perry's parking lot and then back out on US 13, where it pulled to the shoulder. I approached the driver and asked for his driver's license, but he started patting himself down, then looked at me and said, "I left it on my bicycle."

I asked him to get out of the car and into my patrol car. He told me again about leaving his operator's license on his bike.

I sent him back to his car and asked his passenger to return to my vehicle. Even at 1 a.m., it was humid, and as he got in, I said, "It's hot."

The passenger looked at me and said, "Yeah, we got it at the Dodge place."

I got out and arrested him for stealing the car. Then I went to the driver, who realized what was happening. I started to cuff him, and he tried to fight. I was able to cuff him and put him in the car.

The two had stolen the car from the Dodge Place in Emporia, Virginia. As they went through Franklin, Virginia, they broke into a store, stealing change left in the register, cigarettes, and candy. The driver's uncle was on death row, and he told me he wanted to be there also. I guess he thought fame and notoriety existed in that statement.

While stationed in Gates County, there was an outstanding commercial for Timex watches. *It took a licking and kept on ticking.*

A diver was jumping from a tree when he hit a stump under the water and died. He had been underwater for about a week. When his body was found, he was wearing a Timex watch, which was still working fine, even though he had been underwater.

The Chowan River extends ¼ to ½ miles as it winds between Gates County and Hertford County towards the coast.

One night, while I was training young Trooper Mark Brown, we were called to the Chown River bridge. While Mark was measuring the bridge's width, we heard someone screaming from under the bridge in the water, approximately 25 feet down. Mark saw a man with his arms wrapped around the bridge piling. He screamed to the water, asking the man in the water how he had gotten there. Mark asked the man,

"Where is your car? The man replied, "It's in the parking lot at the end of the bridge on the Winton side. Mark replied, "There was no car involved over there." The man replied, "I know I was going to commit suicide, and I changed my mind about halfway down." Mark sent a rescue boat out to get the man, and he was admitted to the Roanoke Chowan Hospital for mental treatment.

The Chowan River in Gates County is a beautiful place. Wildlife is abundant, and in the summer, there are many boats and swimmers—so many that some need to remember about safety. While swimming, a boat can run over a swimmer and cut them in half if the boat driver is unaware of their surroundings. I never investigated this type of accident because the NC Game Wardens have jurisdiction over the waters and rivers, but I saw many similar accidents while stationed in Gates County.

Despite these dangers, I couldn't understand why more people didn't flock to Gates County for a retirement community It was only about an hour from the cities of Norfolk, Virginia, Virginia Beach, and Chesapeake and only about an hour from Kitty Hawk and Manteo, North Carolina It was only two hours from Greenville, North Carolina, and 30 minutes from Edenton and Elizabeth City and Ahoskie, Murfreesboro, depending on where you were in the county, but usually anywhere was a great place. More people would only mean more shopping and more opportunities for more community benefits such as better fire and rescue and better police, instead of just two sheriffs in the Sheriff's office and few doctors and volunteer Rescue and Fire Departments as was the case.

One bright spot in 1978 was the school system in Gates County. That year, Gates County started an immersion program teaching French, and many classes have become foreign languages just because of that program.

Working in Gates County was tough because often, even when you were off, people would come to your house or call you personally if an accident occurred. One morning, at about five am, Mr. Smith called me at my house and told me a car had driven through his cider trees where his chickens were roosting. When Mr. Smith saw this, he shot at the people in the car, and they fled on foot, going about two miles away to the Askew farm, where a one-ton truck was parked under the barn shelter.

They started the truck engine and pulled out from under the barn. When the two Askew boys jumped up on the running board and held guns to their heads until they stopped the trucks and surrendered to them. The Askew boys then called 911 and spoke to someone in Winton.

When I left Mr. Smith's and traveled to the Askew's, I had no idea what was happening, but the Askew boys had it all laid out for me when I got there. I cuffed the guys stealing the truck and took them to the magistrate's office for a bond hearing. This was one morning that I was glad to be off work because Mr. Smith had shot at these guys. I figured I had better go even if I was off that day.

Working in Gates County, you could never tell whom you might see or what might happen. One night, at about 2 A.M., I stopped Duke Assistant Basketball Coach Mike Bray. He was speeding, and while it wasn't much, it was enough to get my attention. He was traveling south on US 13, and when I stopped him, he told me he had been to Pennsylvania on a recruitment trip. He was polite until I asked him for his license.

He began patting his clothes as if looking for his driver's license. Then he looked at the woman who was in the front seat and asked her where his fucking license was? A little girl was seated in the back seat, and the woman appeared uneasy about his language. After several more profanity-laced questions, I asked Mr. Bray to return to my car. Once inside my car, I asked, "Mr. Bray, Is that your wife? "Of course," the answer was yes. "Is that your daughter?" Again, the answer was "Yes." "Well," I said, "If you don't respect them, who do you think will?"

Coach Bray seemed ashamed and dumbfounded as to what to say. He sincerely apologized. Then he told me to contact him if I ever wanted to see a Duke basketball game, which agitated me, but I overlooked it. I issued him a warning ticket and sent him on his way. He was no better or worse than some I had seen, but profanity was what I had witnessed on TV by his boss, Coach K. I didn't feel like seeing or hearing that kind of behavior that night, much less in front of a woman. I think women usually need protection from such language.

A friend of mine in Gates County, Waverly Hollowell, whom I called "Plucket" because he was a carpenter, was lying on his sofa in his living room when suddenly he had a massive craving for a soda pop. He stood up, and as he did, a truck set of tires fell through his ceiling onto the sofa, where he had just seconds before been lying.

The tires had come off a truck traveling north on NC 32. They struck an oak tree in his yard, went airborne, and crashed through his roof, coming down on his sofa.

Within a week, a similar incident happened on US 13, where a set of tires came off the truck and rolled through the parking lot, striking a car parked in the lot.

Late calls were a consistent problem working in Gates County. Every other week, you worked late and took calls. If you worked the morning shift, they would call you early. That meant you were called out at night after or before your morning shift.

I received a call about the Winton Bridge freezing over. Within minutes, I received another radio call that several cars had collided on the bridge. The bridge is ¼ miles across the Chowan River, separating Hertford from Gates County.

When I arrived at the bridge, I found Trooper Wayne Johnson from Hertford County had already arrived. He had already begun collecting information about the cars on the Hertford County side. Winton Bridge was icing up, and the vehicles had slipped into each other's paths. I began collecting information about the cars on the Gates County side of the bridge. I had just seen a car earlier that night and issued the driver a citation for speeding.

I went to the car to look in, and the steering wheel fell out on the bridge when I opened the door. The Rescue Squad had already transported the wounded driver to Roanoke Chowan Hospital in Ahoskie. I finished just before daybreak. Wayne and I went to the hospital to talk to the drivers.

As I approached the driver of the car in which the steering wheel had fallen out, I noticed that both his legs were up in chains, indicating to me that he had two broken legs. I told him Charles H. Jenkin's wrecker service in Ahoskie had his car, and he could go by and look at it when he got out of the hospital. Then, he asked me a question that left me dumbfounded. "Can I drive it home?" he asked. "Sure," I said. "If you can find that steering wheel, drive it home," and I left.

Several months later, I was called back to the bridge for another accident after dark. This time, I was training a new trooper. Mark Brown had been assigned to me for training, and we took the accidents together. When we arrived, Mark heard screaming from off the bridge's western side and walked over to that side, shining his flashlight down to the water. The bridge was approximately ¼ mile across from Gates County to Hertford County, and from top to bottom, it stood about 25 feet above the water.

Mark saw a man holding onto one of the pylons that supported the bridge and hollered to ask him which car he was driving. The man screamed, "The car at the Ahoskie edge of the bridge." Mark replied, "There was no car at the Ahoskie edge involved in the accident." The man yells, "I know. I was going to commit suicide and changed my mind before I hit the water." He walked to the middle of the bridge and jumped but changed his mind before striking the water.

Mark called a rescue boat, and they went out and had the man committed for treatment. Working in Gates County, I found that sometimes, you never know what you might hear or see.

On another day, I stopped a man I called a friend. His

wife was suing him for a divorce when she heard he had a girlfriend. Jimmy was a proud country farmer who lived in a big two-story house with manicured lawns on the Chowan River. While traveling to the office one day, I clocked Jimmy speeding and put the lights on him.

His Ford truck with the dog box and hunting seat pulled over to the side of the road, and Jimmy, all 6 feet from him, exited his vehicle and ran back to me. Jimmy looked at me before I could speak, and with kitten eyes, he said, "Quinn, I got the weight of the world on my shoulders." I gave Jimmy a warning ticket and sent him on his way. From then on, as long as I was in Gates County, when I went to a place Jimmy was at, he would always meet me at the door. Jimmy expressed his gratitude by greeting me at the door and welcoming me inside. While living, one day, we lost him and couldn't find him. We asked Travis if he knew where Rusty was. There was no answer, so I went around my neighborhood and called on the PA system for him. I could not find the poodle, which cost a lot of money. Tiny is smaller than miniature dogs. Travis said he knew where he was. With that, he led us to a desk in his room. I opened up the desk drawer, and there lay Rusty asleep.

Sherry and I would go home to visit my parents. It was, at best, a 2–3-hour drive, depending on where we were going, either to Trenton to my parents or Wilson to hers. We would keep the boys occupied by singing songs. One song we liked to sing, and they became very good at, was Dead Skunk in the Middle of the Road.

We found that Bret had become immersed in religion or my dad's view of religion. Over the years, I found that Dad's view of religion was not precisely biblical.

I had a subscription to Playboy Magazine. Back then, the magazine featured nude models. The magazines were kept in the top of a closet in the bedroom. Once, Sherry and I caught Travis sitting on the sofa in our living room, looking at a naked model on the pages. The magazine had fallen on the floor in the closet. Travis would go searching for things. That is how he found the magazine.

I stopped a pickup truck with a camper shell on the back for speeding. It looked like everything the owner had was in the truck. When I approached the driver and explained why I stopped him. I asked him to meet me at my car. As he sat in the front seat of my car, he began to cry.

"Sir, you can give me a ticket, but I can't afford it. I've had a heart attack, and I've lost everything I own. We will live with my cousin in Maysville, NC because I have lost my home."

I told him to wait there and went to the passenger side of the old Ford Truck. There, I saw his wife with tears rolling down her checks. I tapped on the window, and she said when she'd rolled it down.

"Sir, you can give him a ticket, but we can't afford it. He just had a heart attack, and we have lost everything we own. We are visiting Maysville, NC, to stay with his cousin."

I returned to the patrol car, issued him a warning ticket, and gave him my dad's number. I told him my dad lived down there and had just had a heart attack and would love to help him with that; I sent them on their way.

I may go to hell for being a cold, violent butt, but I refuse to face my God with the accusation that I did not care for my fellow man.

Sometimes, being on the Highway Patrol caused personal issues for my family. Case in point: My father-in-law was a salesman for Swift Foods in Wilson. One day, a salesman for Dinner Bell Foods came into his office and, knowing him, looked at him and said, "Walker, I got a ticket."

His exact words were, "I got a ticket from a redheaded SOB Trooper." My father-in-law asked him where he got the ticket, and he replied, "In Gates County." To that, my father-in-law said, "That red-headed SOB is my son-in-law."

While working in Gates County, I was investigated for what was called "making too many drug arrests." The Highway Patrol told me that if I accepted this transfer, there would be no charges against me, and I gladly accepted. They sent me to drug interdiction school, and I was getting 90% pure cocaine, but I still left without argument. 90% pure means that after the drug has been mixed to lower the pure content of the cocaine, it was still 90% pure cocaine.

Simply put, there are two people in a county that, when they file a complaint, will get a trooper moved: one is the district attorney, and the other is the Sheriff. I was given a stack of openings in the state, and I asked to go to Wayne County. At the time, I knew District Attorney Donald Jacobs was in Wayne County and could trust him. When I arrived in Wayne County, I explained to Don what had happened. I told him of a call I had gotten from the Elizabeth City DA when he said I was making too many drug arrests.

Jacobs explained that he would go to the DA's conference, and the District Attorney would complain that he could not get his officers to make drug arrests. He told me how the brother of that District Attorney had been arrested while driving the DA's car in a reverse sting in Greenville. He said he now understood what was happening. A few months later, the District Attorney in Elizabeth City lost his job to an assistant in his office, and it was good to me.

I knew Jacobs from Greene County and trusted him beyond measure. When he retired, I had already retired from the Patrol. While eating lunch at Wilbur's Bar-B-Que, I called Jacobs, telling my friend Wilber Shirley that Jacobs was retiring. Jacobs didn't need to represent drug dealers that he had sent to prison. Within a few weeks, the Governor had appointed Jacobs as a special Superior Court Judge.

Chapter Seven: Working Wayne County

Wayne County was the complete opposite of Gates County. This county had approximately 100,000 people, unlike Gates, which had only 8000 people.

Wayne County had a modern Sheriff's office with approximately 100 employees instead of one Sheriff and one deputy like Gates. Wayne had a well-staffed jail, unlike Gates, where you had to transport prisoners to another County. Wayne County had a well-funded hospital, several dozen doctor's offices, and a well-established rescue squad that was usually on the scene of an accident when you arrived.

Wayne County had Seymour Johnson Air Force Base, comprising a large land mass and hundreds of government offices with military employees and their dependents. Wayne County had a daily newspaper and a television station, whereas Gates County newspapers came out only on Wednesdays.

During the Bosnian War, Wayne County had dependents entering in a large mass. The leading number of people entering Wayne County was, in fact, from Bosnia, whereas Gates County had few people coming into that county at all to stay.

Besides that, Wayne County offers some resources perfect for law enforcement. Unlike Onslow County, where Camp Lejeune is located, few Air Force personnel are involved in acts of violence on the road. They are trained for discipline and respect and usually obey direct orders from civil authority or military leadership. They rarely fight with law enforcement. My friends stationed at Camp Lejeune told me they spent a lot of time fighting Marines, but I never had to fight an airman from Seymour Johnson.

Calls for assistance were usually answered in 5 minutes or

less because police officers were in every significant town within the county.

There were 1,000 different reasons to choose Wayne County over Gates County, including the opportunity for myself after retirement. I was glad to come here.

Wayne County had a massive court system, with court held every day instead of just one day every two weeks in Gates County. The heads of the district courts, judges, district judges, and district attorneys from three counties were established in Wayne County.

Instead of working in three counties, sometimes alone, there were 18 Troopers in Wayne County. Usually, there were 3 or 4 working together on a shift.

Occasionally, I had to work alone, but it was rare. If I got myself in trouble, there were always deputies and police officers nearby.

In addition to the usual duties of the Highway Patrol in Wayne County, I was permanently assigned to special assignments, such as school or football games. Even when the governor wanted a Highway Patrol presence, whether for additional security or a media presence, I was sent to the event.

I also had more opportunities to provide security for more dignitaries than I typically could in Gates County. Through my friend Wilber Shirley, I met many well-known people like President Bill Clinton, Governors Terry Sanford, and Beverly Purdue. I also met and became close friends with Lt. Governor Dennis Wicker and Republican I. Beverly Lake, the NC Supreme Court Chief Justice and the majority leader of the NC House, Philip Baddour, Jr., soon became a friend.

My old First Sergeant from Ahoskie, Jim Minton, called and started to tell Sherry that he was sorry about my death. Sherry told him that I was not dead but was outside cutting grass. After speaking with me, Minton had to contact the First Sergeant in Goldsboro to send a car to my home to verify that I had not been shot and killed. It was a rumor that someone in Gates County had started months after we moved, but it still had to be checked out.

Dennis Williams, another Trooper stationed in Wayne with me, and I were going to court. We came upon a stranded vehicle broken down at the intersection of William and Ash Streets. He and I pushed his car off the road and into the BB&T Bank parking lot. This was on Thursday, and I couldn't get out of bed by Sunday. Sherry assisted me by getting me to the hospital, where I was informed that I needed emergency surgery. During the surgery, the surgeon found that a portion had already turned into gang green and removed it.

I joined the Police Benevolent Association (PBA), an association of police officers in the Southern States with representation and support in Congress. I worked to lobby for police rights, as unions are forbidden in North Carolina. This group also lobbied in the state legislature for police officers and offered legal representation for those who believed they were unjustly punished or terminated.

I worked inside the PBA, even while employed by the Highway Patrol. I was appointed by President Jeff Fluck, a Raleigh Police homicide detective who was state President for the N.C. Division. I eventually became a legislative liaison person and joined President Fluck in lobbying inside the Legislature for policy issues.

I ran and was elected by the Troopers of North Carolina to be President of the Highway Patrol Chapter. I created a formal governing board of that chapter, including Troopers to Majors. As the President, I followed the direction of that board meeting monthly to discuss Patrol issues. Commissioned Officers did not sway the board members, but we voted our conscience as we viewed the issues.

The board members supported each other, and the commissioned and noncommissioned officers made the best recommendations we could to the Highway Patrol. I also wrote a piece on law enforcement for the PBA magazine, which is published and distributed in the Southeast United States.

We held screening boards for state and federal candidates to garner endorsements from the PBA. As president, I received calls from politicians from across the state who wanted our support to train them on what to expect from board members when being questioned.

In addition, I started getting calls from those who requested my support in getting issues passed for the Patrol in the legislature. When I asked for permission to work on my days off for the PBA, the commander of the Highway Patrol allowed it, which he rarely allowed others to do.

On my days off, I traveled the state recruiting new members for the PBA, and as such, I became more influential as a leader across the state. Troopers all across the state knew me and asked my advice on issues.

As President, the PBA directed me to decide whether a PBA lawyer should represent someone who claimed they were wrongly accused of a policy violation or terminated. I would contact the PBA legal staff and request aid. I took that very seriously, and while you may say I was determining innocence or guilt without a trial, I was following PBA guidelines.

Sometimes, I asked for help, but sometimes, I had to reject an appeal. I refused when the evidence was clear that the person had violated policy.

I was happy when I retired and began my rest period. After 30 years as a law enforcement officer, I was ready. Few people retire at 49 years old, and even fewer in my family are healthy and have made a good life for themselves and their families at that age. I have a college degree, which I obtained while in law enforcement. My boys both had received college degrees and had good jobs. As a result of my career in law enforcement, I even learned a foreign language, Spanish.

My First Sergeant in Wayne County, at the time, was very difficult to comprehend. On Sundays, he worked a 1 pm to 10 pm shift, and instead of going on the road, he would sit in his office with his hands on his desk. If I went in to see him in February and said Sergeant, my birthday is October 27th, and I'd like to be off. He would look it up on the schedule, which he did for the entire year in January, and said I was working on the 27th, and then he would refuse to give me off.

Things were so bad that we only wrote the minimum number of tickets we could get by with on my shift. The minimum refers to what is expected from each Trooper. We would go to a secret location behind a business and stay most of the shift to avoid the supervisors. The First Sergeant took pictures of the men and placed them on the office walls. If someone came in to complain, he would point at the pictures and ask which person it was. He never cared to defend us. He just wanted to punish us. When he retired, his farewell party had to be moved to another county because the men would not participate. Only two in our district attended his retirement and were on the promotion list.

When I first got to Wayne County, I had to set the record straight on what I would take from the locals. They didn't know me, and I didn't know them. Some wanted to get by with the minimum safety procedures. They did what they needed to do regarding accidents when acting as volunteer firefighters.

For example, one accident occurred while working on Pecan Road in Wayne County. This road goes down a steep grade over a bridge and back up the grade on the other side.

In this particular situation, I was working on an accident where a car had run off the road and down the ravine. The wrecker pulled up to pull the car out, and a volunteer fireman went down into the ravine with the wrecker's cable. After getting the car hooked up, the fireman began riding the car back up the hill. I stopped the wrecker driver cold in his tracks and told him to advise the fireman to return up the hill. Then, we would pull the car up the hill after him. The fireman objected and said, "I'm fine. Go ahead."

"No," I said. "You come up, and we will pull up the car."

Again, the fireman protested, saying, "I'm fine; pull up the car." I stopped the wrecker driver and told the fire chief to either bring his fireman up the hill or he could take his whole department back to the firehouse, and I would get another Fire Department to work this accident. At that point, the Chief directed his man to come up, and he did. If that cable had broken while he was riding that car and he died or was injured, I would never have been able to buy a drink for myself because he or his family would have sued me, and the Highway Patrol would have fired me.

After going to Wayne County, I became friends with Lt. Governor Dennis Wicker. We were so close that I believe that had he won the governor's election, I would have had a better chance for a promotion. He lost the election, and the rest is history. Then, the promotion process was political, probably more so than it is today.

My good friend Wilber Shirley made sure I met several influential politicians, one of whom was Phil Baddour, the majority leader in the State House. Phil Baddour was a native of Wayne County and was close to Governor James B. Hunt, Jr. One day, he asked me who we needed for Colonel of the Highway Patrol. I told him we needed Richard Holden. Holden was black and would be the first Black Commander of the Highway Patrol, which would help Hunt when he ran again. In two weeks, Governor Hunt's office announced Richard Holden's placement as the new Commander of the Highway Patrol.

After Holden served and had died, a friend of mine, Jack Smith, also black, who served as my Lieutenant and earlier as my First Sergeant in Wayne County, told me Holden had denied him a Captain's position because, as Jack put it, Holden thought Smith was an Uncle Tom. I have known Jack Smith for a long time and can honestly say there is no better person. He treats people as well as they will allow him to. He has never forgotten where he came from, and I regret telling Phil Baddour that Holden was the right person for that job.

I had an excellent relationship with Holden, and although

I never personally told him I had pushed for his promotion, I benefited greatly from it.

In Wayne County, I met a Cuban man named Gasper Gonzales. Gasper had been captured in Vietnam. He was born in the United States but raised in Cuba and joined the US military. After the war, he was a CIA Agent working, as he described it, to cause unrest in some South and Central American countries and to stabilize others. Gasper taught me Spanish. We became closer. When I was nominated for US Marshal by Senator Kay Hagen, I told Gasper that I did not know anyone outside North Carolina. He got me a recommendation from Senator Bob Menendez from New Jersey. One day, in the snow and ice, Gasper slipped and broke his spine and later died in a nursing home. Gasper received three bronze stars while in the military and was a great man as far as I am concerned.

Another person I was close to was a black woman named Deloris Kennedy. I met Mrs. Kennedy while chairing the Democratic Party in Wayne County. I told her I had no one outside of North Carolina to help me get the support of President Obama. She called a childhood friend whom she had dated from Harlem, New York, Congressman Charlie Rangel.

A few days after we talked, I got a call from the Congressman's office in DC while in Gene Riddle's law office. Gene was a civil lawyer I worked for after I retired from The Highway Patrol and was good to work for. The lady asked me to send my resume to Rangel's office, and I did.

The next evening, at about 7 p.m., I got another call. This time, a man said, "Were we supposed to deliver your information to the President?" I, of course, said, "Yes," and he said, "Well, it's been done." Well, I didn't get picked, but I tried, and for that, I am proud.

When I first went to Wayne County, I started coaching baseball for kids on my days off. I coached the thirteen-year-olds and was elected to the board as the Babe Ruth Baseball League representative. I was so proud when my team from Spring Creek won first place in the district tournament. We went to Wilmington for the State Tournament, but it was as if the players we were up against were twenty-one-year-olds. Each had been hand-picked by the Raleigh team we played against. Each time they stepped to the plate, their players hit a home run. I was fatigued trying to win and disgusted with how they were playing. Things only got worse as I got food poisoning and, after the game, had to go to the hospital.

Working in Wayne County was a big plus, but there were negatives. I learned early on that being close to a base like Seymour Johnson Air Force Base has advantages. For instance, a friend of mine worked on the base and had a connection. He would ensure I had the latest equipment, like first aid equipment. This was usually better equipment than what the Highway Patrol supplied us with.

There were other negatives, too. One night, I discovered the downside when an Osprey from Cherry Point crashed before landing just short of the base. It was a Sunday Night when both Trooper Butch Dillard and I were working. Butch told me we needed to stand by the plane until the Security Police got to the plane site.

When I say plane, I mean a jet armed with God only knows what kinds of weapons. The crash site was about a mile from the Parkstown Community in Northeastern Wayne County.

When we arrived at the site, we found the pilot dangling by his parachute about 10 feet above the ground from a tree he had gotten caught in. The pilot advised us that the plane was about 100 yards behind him in the woods. We were able to find what was left of it burning there.

All of a sudden, the guns started firing, or at least bullets began exploding, and like the comic strip I had seen during the war, a kid in Vietnam spoke, saying he gladly would hide if he had only known which side of the tree was safe.

Almost immediately, local farmers came through the woods, some walking, some on four-wheelers. We had to ask them to leave.

For almost an hour, I wished I had not gone because I never knew when a bomb would blow, but Butch had been in the county a lot longer than me, and I figured he knew what to do.

On another occasion, just before Desert Storm, a guy in Jones County stole a truck belonging to a friend of mine, Randy Foy. A trooper jumped him, and he went on a wild goose chase through Lenior, Greene, and Wayne Counties.

I picked up the chase at Pinewood, and we went down Berkley Blvd. and into Seymour Johnson Air Force Base. The base had no defensive barricades, so the pickup driver drove through the main gate and down the street, crossing the tarmac where the big planes took off and landed.

As soon as we entered the gates, the Security Police notified the tower, and the jets were rerouted elsewhere. They were either told to fly around or go to another base. At the pistol range, located at the back of the base, the truck tried to cross some small ditches and got stuck. It was there he was arrested. We had put the cuffs on him before the Security Police even arrived.

In 2000, being on the Highway Patrol created a problem for my friends, family, and myself. When the whole world was off for Christmas, the Highway Patrol, depending on your luck, had to work Christmas. Only half of the state got to be off at Christmas. Those unlucky ones had the week before Christmas, but we all worked on New Year because of the Y2K concerns, which was a nothing burger, no substance there.

And there were good times, too. On one occasion, Sergeant Jack Smith authorized a district softball game to be played at the Nahunta Baseball Complex. I was a catcher for our team. There was this one time when the ball was thrown, and I completely lost it. When I stood up, the ball fell from my long shorts.

Jack Smith was made Lieutenant, and, as far as I'm concerned, he should have been Colonel, but as I said earlier, he was stopped by someone I helped get the commander's position. Jack retired from the Patrol and became Chief Deputy in Nash County before running and becoming Sheriff in Northampton County.

One night, Erskine Bowles called me at home. I remembered his dad, Skipper Bowles, running for Governor. I was the Legislative Chief for the NC Chapter of the PBA, and someone had recommended that he call me even though we had never met before that night. I had never even talked to him. He called me and said, "Bronnie, this is Erskine Bowles." The only way I knew him then was his connection with the Clinton Administration and his being Bill Clinton's Chief of Staff. At that time, he was running for the US Senate against Republican Libby Dole. The next day, he had an interview with the PBA to gain support for his campaign.

"Bronnie," he said, "I need your support tomorrow. I have to meet with the PBA for their endorsement, and I was hoping you could help me get acquainted with that process. Can you do that?"

I always planned to vote for him anyway and answered that I could. The next day, he sat near me. When it was my time to question him, I asked him a tricky question. "Mr. Bowles," I said, "When you were at the White House, did anyone ever mention Roswell, New Mexico?" You could have heard a pin drop, and suddenly he laughed, realizing it was a 'give me question, and said, "No, Bronnie, no one ever did."

He received our endorsement with my help and much more support than I knew then but was ultimately defeated in the election.

Six years later, he ran again, but this time, I had retired. He held a rally at Wilbers restaurant. I went and just stood back, thinking he would never remember me. When Erskine entered the door, the crowd stood waiting for him to shake hands. Soon, he was free from that reception line. Suddenly, I saw Erskine Bowles walking over with his hands stretched to me, saying, "Hi, Bronnie Quinn."

skine. I was in the middle of the US
like it was my last hope. It was not
f my last hopes. I called Erskine
and he answered the phone as
arlier. I explained why I called
oort. Erskine remembered me
morrow." I can't say he did or
told me he would, and I believe

out the 27th of December, I got a call from my
ner-in-law, who told me he was at Dicks Hot Dog Stand
in Wilson. Mr. Lee Gliarmis, the owner of Dicks Hotdogs,
was a friend of the family, and it was not unusual to hear
he was there. What surprised me was whom he had called
for. Water Jones Jr. was there and had told him he would
help me. Congressman Walter Jones and I were friends
even though Walter had become a Republican and I was a
Democrat. We had been friends for many years. Walter's
dad, a Democrat, and I were good friends when I lived at
Cobbs Crossroads in Greene County. I often saw him in
Farmville.

Walter told me he would return to Washington on the 3rd of
January, but for me to call him at his Farmville home the
weekend after that.

I called his home, and he told me something greatly
distressed me. "Bronnie," he said, "Things are so bad in
Washington right now that if I tell them I support you,
it will hurt you, so I'm just gonna be quiet." I thanked
him and understood I had heard the same from others. It
was disheartening that Democrats and Republicans can't
agree on anything because our government requires them
to work together and compromise to get things done.

In any case, I did not get the appointment. It would have
been sweet, but that is how things were, and I understood.
I was blessed to be nominated and even more blessed to
have been considered. As the Congressman explained, if
the country had forgotten how things like that were going
in Washington, I would have been even more fortunate *not*

to have gotten it.

With everything Wayne County had going for it, it [...]
to be upset about being transferred here. Somet[...]
would get depressed. Then, usually, I would think abo[...]
the friends I had made here over the years—all the frie[...]
in Greene and Gates counties, as well as other friends[...]
had made growing up in Jones County. The memories[...]
usually brought me back to reality.

Friendship is the main reason for existence. I am so lucky
to have people in my life. I consider myself a good friend
and have had many good friends, such as Wilber and
Emmitt Fields.

Emmitt had a massive heart attack shortly after I got here,
and I even gave him CPR, but I could not save him.

Lee Roy Talton and Ed Coors were my friends, too. I
thought the sun rose and sat in Lee Roy. When we moved
into our mobile home, a wind shear turned it over. I looked
up, and Lee Roy was crawling around under the trailer. I
remember him telling my dad what to do as it was being
set back up.

I asked Dad, "Do you know him?"

He replied, "I thought you did."

I looked at Dad and said, "We better listen to him. He may
be from Cherry Hospital," but he was there daily helping
us and never charged me a dime.

Mr. Gordan Best of Best Sand and Gravel sent his front-
end loader, and George Humphrey sent two wreckers,
lifted my mobile home, sat it right, and never sent me a
bill. One day after I built my new stick house, Mr. Gordan
came to see me. He told me he was a millionaire, and I
said I never met a millionaire before. He said, well, I own a
million buckets of sand, which ought to be worth a dollar
a bucket.

Lee Roy and I became terrific friends. One night, he came
to see me. He began to tell me that they had charged him.
If you knew Lee Roy, you figured someone had sent him a

bill when he said things like that. However, it was much more complex than that.

Lee Roy explained that he was mowing the grass at his son's home, and a girl brought him a glass of water. When a neighbor saw this, she called to him to stop molesting that little girl. As customary in the South, Lee Roy hugged the girl to thank her. Lee Roy swore to me that what he was accused of had never happened. Soon afterward, the sheriff came and arrested him. Within weeks, Lee Roy became so sad and embarrassed by the incident that he killed himself. I lost a very dear friend that day.

Ed Coor lived across from Lee Roy. He and I soon became good friends, too. I would help Ed with his hay field when the hay was cut and baled. We talked about many things. Ed became a good friend, and he is gone now, also.

1996 Hurricane Fran struck North Carolina, the worst economic disaster ever recorded. Hurricane-force winds blew inland as far as Raleigh. The flooding was devastating to Wayne County. In all, over 4 million acres in North Carolina were flooded. Fifty-seven people died in total, with 35 coming from just North Carolina.

I was assigned a traffic stop checkpoint on NC111 at Mrs. Margaret Grady's home. I was to stop traffic and send it back north. The bridges were closed at the Neuse River and along US 70 to the east. The bridges on US 117 across the Neuse River were flooded. There were trees all across the roads in North Carolina.

Around 11 o'clock that first night, a truck pulling a boat came down the road, stopping at the checkpoint. The occupants told me they were en route to Seven Springs, a small village in Eastern Wayne County. The small town is located along the Neuse River. They also told me they wanted to help the people of Seven Springs evacuate. Having lived in that section of the county and knowing those people had been evacuated for a week, I quickly decided to have them turn around and send them back to Goldsboro. My son, Bret, had gone to help people from Seven Springs evacuate a week before this, and all had safely gotten out.

Pretty soon, a female in a pickup truck entered the checkpoint and told me she had to get to Camp Lejeune Marine Corps Base; I courteously explained to her that the roads were closed due to the bridges being in danger of washing out at the Neuse River on NC111, on US 117, and at the creeks on US 70 in Lenoir County.

She said, "You're not listening to me. She said, "I HAVE to get to Camp Lejeune."

And with that, I again explained. "Yes, madame, I heard you, but you did not hear me; you *cannot* drive to Camp Lejeune."

Again, she yelled, "You didn't hear me!"

Again, I said, "Yes, Ma'am, you're right; I'm sorry, I now understand you. Are you familiar with Seymour Johnson Air Force Base?"

She anxiously said, "Yes, I am."

"Are you familiar with how to get to the front Gate," I asked her.

"Yes," she said. "Go there," I said. "When you reach the front gate, ask for the General in charge. Are you with me so far?" I asked her.

"Yes, of course," she said.

"When he comes, you tell him you need one of his airplanes because you cannot drive to Camp Lejeune!" I yelled.

She was so mad. She just turned around and returned to Goldsboro. I never saw her again. Luckily, I didn't get a complaint.

Later, a trooper from Wilkes County and I got a break while the National Guard watched the traffic. We drove down St. Johns Church Road to the creek, where the bridge had already been washed out. Suddenly, an alligator-type animal floated by, and I asked him if he saw that snake.

He replied, "That was no snake; that was a gator."

Later, we were moved to the intersection of NC111 and St. John Church Road near my home. At around 10 p.m., a car pulled up and pulled off the road, and the driver came walking up to me.

"Sir," the young boy said, "Can you explain how I can get to Grantham? My wife is pregnant, and we went to the hospital, but they released us, and we can't get back home."

Again, I explained how all the bridges were nearly washed out. Roads were closed all over the county, and the best thing he could do was return to Goldsboro and find a motel room for the night; then, maybe he could find a way home tomorrow. He seemed in despair as he explained that he had no money for a room.

I had my cell phone and called my wife. We lived about ½ miles back from the road in the woods. Our sons were away at college, so we had two extra rooms. I told her to drive to the end of our road to meet the couple, and we would have guests for the night. As she did that, I explained to the young man to follow my wife, and they could stay there for the night for free. He followed her to our home, went in, and spent the night.

The following day, I got in about 6 am after my shift and went to bed. By 7:30, my wife awakened me and told me our guests were already gone. To that, I just told her to check the silver and make sure nothing was gone and went back to sleep,

I have never seen such flooding between Hurricanes Fran and Floyd in Wayne County. The state needed more detour and direction signs, so people made more signs using plywood and paint.

As I have said, raising the boys was the most challenging thing I ever did. Travis was just like me. I knew he was like me, and he was just as sneaky, too. Once, he hid on the roof overlooking the walkway to our door. As I came up the walk, he peed on me. I thought it was rain and just ignored it. When Travis got to college in Wilmington, he partied too much and let his studies go, just like I had done.

He called me and said, "Dad, I don't think I will graduate."

I answered, "Son, you are going to graduate. You may be 40 years old before you do, but you will graduate."

Of course, I couldn't keep him in college until he was 40. Still, he knew I meant that he would remain in college until he graduated as long as he lived with me. He would eat and stay at my house until he graduated, which was something he never wanted to have happen.

Sherry went shopping with Travis and her mother one Saturday to Raleigh. Travis' grades were slipping, and when her mother asked about them, he had to tell her what he had been up to. Her mother was not very happy with him. Sherry told her not to give him one dime. He would call her if he needed anything, so until his grades improved, he didn't receive any money from her.

Bret, on the other hand, was the opposite person. He graduated with a 3.7 grade point average four years after starting college. He had a job waiting at Goldsboro Milling after finishing school. Bret worked for Goldsboro Milling Company doing computer programming. He loved it and worked there for about eight years. He built a new home and married within a few weeks of graduation. He would have stayed, but the mill appeared to be in decline. A local bank hired him to ensure computer program certifications were current. He could work from home with the position.

Although the oldest, Travis graduated the semester after Bret and started an internship at Walt Disney World in Florida within a few weeks. Travis went to Disney and loved it for the duration. However, Disney was not keen on paying. The money they gave interns would be taken back for transportation and living expenses. After just a few months of internship, Travis told Disney he would return to Wilmington and home if they didn't have a more profitable job.

As I said, being a parent was not easy, but being a parent on the Highway Parol was almost impossible. I was never home, and when they had sporting events, which Sherry wisely kept them involved in, I had to take my meal hour to see them. If their sports took them out of the county, I would often miss them because I was working.

I wore out two cars, sending Sherry to sporting events. With Travis in baseball and all-conference and Bret in wrestling and all-conference, somehow and someway, they stayed out of trouble for the most part.

There was that one time with each. Travis decided to go around on Halloween with a group of boys and knock down mailboxes. When he got caught, they had to visit the local jail. That trip to the jail with the inmates scared him straight.

Bret got caught speeding at 80 mph in a 55 mph zone. If a friend of mine had not seen him, he would have lost his license for 30 days. However, the friend allowed me to punish him, and I took his license for 30 days. **What does this mean?** He had to put his license on the television and leave them there for 30 days.

Recently, with the attempted assassination of former President Donald Trump, I was reminded of the security details I worked for Presidents. I worked with Ronald Regan immediately after the Challenger exploded and with Vice President Quail once. I was eating dinner with my family when Bill Clinton, as a candidate, stopped by. I remember being asked about my gun by the Secret Service.

Reagan came down to Havelock to Cherry Hospital to speak, and we were told we could neither confirm he was coming nor deny it. I was assigned an intersection outside of Newport where Regan would pass. There were two motorcycles from the Highway Patrol, two or three SUVs, two Limos with the Presidential seal on each side, several SUVs all armed by Secret Service agents, and more Troopers cars and motorcycles. Above the caravan flew Huey helicopters with a gunner on each side, with Machine Guns swerving around, looking for a target.

I remember a woman approaching me and asking if the

President was coming down that day. As I was instructed, I told her I could not deny or confirm.

She replied well, I know that he is coming. I talked to him last night. I know he is.

She was the sister of Challenger pilot Michael Smith from Beaufort, NC, and had talked to President Reagan the night before. Still, I had instructions on how to answer and followed them.

Looking at the Kennedy assassination in 1963, we see the commitment of the Secret Service's commitment to protecting the protected. Special Agent Hill threw himself on top of First Lady Jackie Kenndy to protect her, never even thinking about the risk he was presenting for himself.

I worked a lot in security for dignitaries, from governors to presidents, but I was never quite sure I could take a bullet for someone else.

Chapter Eight: Retirement from NCHP

One day after my retirement, I went to the Clerk's Office to check on a case that I had pending. I ran into Gene Riddle, a civil lawyer, here in Goldsboro. Gene stated he wanted me to come by and see him because he wanted to offer me a job.

During the conversation, he directed me to come by on Monday. I did, and he told me about the benefits of working for him. He finished with, "We'll have fun." That is precisely what I have had for over six years.

Gene is a civil attorney, and we only took civil cases. His specialties are accidents and personal injury cases of all kinds.

For instance, one case was a 16-year-old girl who died when she was struck by a truck hauling Chicken guts traveling north on NC111.

The collision occurred on a Monday, and Gene asked me to call the father and help him as much as possible on that Tuesday. I did, and he asked me to prove his daughter did not cause the accident.

I contacted the trooper who investigated the accident, whom I had worked with, and thought he was a good trooper. He explained that he had a witness who stated they were directly behind the gut truck and saw the light change to red before the girl entered the roadway, was struck, and died. He told me he had requested vacation time and was due to leave the following day for a trip to Florida. Having already paid his airfare, he could not put more time into this investigation.

I thanked him and called the District Attorney at his home number. I requested an accident reconstruction from him. I was lucky enough that he requested the reconstruction of the accident from the Highway Patrol. District Attorney

Branny Vickory was a good DA and a good friend. He jumped right in to help me.

I heard a rumor about a young girl at the Western Steer restaurant who had seen the accident. She told me she was behind the two people who said they saw the light from behind the truck. She explained that they were so close to the truck that they could not have seen it over its bed.

After interviewing her, I decided their testimony was wrong and looked further into the evidence.

I hired Reggie Hines, a former DMV Traffic enforcement officer with his company, to obtain traffic information. He had many more contacts in the DMV than I did. He could get me information on the trucking company, such as how often trucks had been stopped and inspected. He also could get information on the drivers that I needed help getting.

I contacted the DOT and asked for a written report on the intersection light and a detailed report on any problems with it since the date of the accident. I also requested a report on whether it worked properly on that date.

I began putting out feelers stating that I was looking for any witness to this collision. A few weeks later, I was sitting at the light and looking at it. Suddenly, I had an epiphany. The truck refused to stop, and I could see the whole accident in slow motion.

I returned to the office and requested permission from Gene Riddle to hire a reconstruction expert. I contacted Kemley-Horn in Cary, a company that reconstructs and helps cities with traffic lights and traffic flow problems. Kemley-Horn reconstructed the accident and told me the truck driver got a yellow light about 700 feet from the intersection. After the yellow warning light, there would have been 400 feet before a collision. He did not stop; therefore, he collided with the girl.

I then spoke to two boys who were in a truck at the intersection going east, opposite the young girl who was killed. They told me it was a hot day. The air conditioner on their pickup truck was not working, and the driver stopped to adjust the air conditioning. Then, they realized that the gut truck was not stopping. The girl who had the green light was entering the intersection. Both boys agreed that if they had proceeded out under the green light, the truck would have killed them, too.

I then found a young girl in a home near the intersection who was taking a bath at the time. She heard the horn blowing several times from the gut truck and heard all this before she heard the car striking the truck. Even though the radio played loudly while she was in the bath, she still heard the truck horn.

The owner of the home where the car and truck came to rest stated that the driver jumped and ran out across her yard into her home, overlooking any help for the young girl in the car. The car caught fire with the girl still inside. The girl, who the autopsy said had been alive, died as a result of the fire and not the collision between the car and gut truck.

I sent my report to the DA, who called and asked why I could get my report in faster than the Highway Patrol Reconstruction Team. When the Highway Patrol's report finally came in, it matched my findings to a tee.

The DA, Branny Vickory, called me to ask what I thought was fair. I told him I felt the driver should be charged with, at minimum, Death by Motor Vehicle. Soon after, he was accused of that and pleaded guilty to it.

But this was not the first death this driver had caused. It was especially unnerving to find that he had caused an accident before and that someone else had died from his careless behavior while driving.

In addition, the trucking company had a long history of violations, including no brakes, no lights, speeding, and other moving violations. Drivers were charged and convicted of all these different violations.

Several months later, he pled to death by vehicle, which

only helped our civil case.

A few months later, the trucking company's insurance company agreed to pay the parents $980,000.00. The parents were worn out from all of it. The insurance company lawyer told a friend of mine that we could have easily gotten $1 million had we pushed for it.

I worked on many civil cases for Gene. These ranged from Personal Injury cases involving slips and falls to falling deaths while working and Workers' compensation cases.

As Gene had predicted and told me, "I had a ball." First, I was paid well. I felt respected for my knowledge, and honestly. I probably would have stayed there longer if I had not been nominated for the US Marshall's position in Eastern NC. Gene thought I had it tied up and hired someone to take my place. I respected his decision but wish he had waited.

I thank Gene Riddle because, when I opened my own company, I would not have had the knowledge to do an excellent job for my clients without a foundation in civil and criminal law.

While working for Riddle, I was allowed to do something I had always wanted, but I was never allowed to do it in law enforcement.

I sought and was elected to the Chairmanship of the Wayne County Democratic Party. There, I met and had access to many of the top state-elected members. I even became friends with many Republicans.

I met President Clinton, Governors Hunt and Perdue, and Governor Easley. I also met Governor Terry Sanford when I helped to celebrate his 80th birthday at Duke University, where he had been President.

I was particularly close to Lt. Governor Dennis Wicker and even got US Senator Kay Hagen to nominate me for US Marshal for the Eastern District of North Carolina. I became friends with Beverly Lake, the State's Chief Justice of the State Supreme Court.

After four years, I opened my own Private investigation business, and since I had clients from both parties, I withdrew from politics in the public sense. You get the government you pay for, meaning the candidates you support need money to get the voters' attention. I believe in getting their attention, so I secretly supported many candidates, including Congressman Don Davis from Snow Hill. I found Don to be above average and had worked his way up. I supported him and still support those reasons.

I heard about Don Davis while working as a young deputy sheriff in Greene County. White deputies I knew and trusted described him as an outstanding young black man. Everything they said about Don Davis was good, and I have found that to be true.

Although I had a good chance at the Marshal's run, I lost. The President of the United States would choose the Marshall. At that time, the President was Obama. President Obama chose Scotty Parker, a Deputy from Nash County. Scotty was a great choice, and I respected that decision.

As I have said, I worked on cases that taught me about civil laws and broadened my horizons of what a Private Investigator should know. While this helped me, it also taught me shortcuts to finding answers and where to go to get those answers.

It introduced me to people I did not know in law enforcement and put me out there as someone people could contact if they had a problem and needed a Private Investigator.

Gene Riddle became a friend and a confidant. If I had a problem, I could count on Gene to provide me with an answer, which usually gave me a solution.

While I was Wayne County Democratic Chair, my good friend Donald Jacobs retired from the District Attorney's Office. I heard about it, and when he passed me in Wilber's Restaurant at lunch, I motioned for him to sit down. Don was the head district attorney and had been the chief reason many people went to prison for drug cases. He was the principal prosecutor in the "Ike Atkinson" case, a federal drug case that was turned over to Jacobs.

Atkinson was stationed in Vietnam and sent drugs back through Seymour Johnson Air Force Base in furniture and was distributed by others in the drug trade. Jacobs's life was threatened, and several prominent drug dealers were imprisoned due to his efforts.

I told him, "Don, you need a friend," I called Wilber Shirley over to our table.

I said, "Don is going to retire, Wilber; he doesn't need to be a lawyer for the drug dealers he has sent to prison. He needs to be a judge".

Within two weeks, the Governor's office announced that Donald Jacobs' would assume a special judgeship upon retirement. That was one of the best outcomes I have ever helped with.

Chapter Nine: Private Investigations

Working for Gene Riddle was great fun, but working for myself, I was constantly worried about building my company. Doing a good job, keeping the business coming in, renewing the licenses, and finding top-notch help.

About a month after I left Riddle & Brantley. Gene had his staff provide my investigation hours for my application for a private investigator license. I needed three thousand hours. While I had that cut in half with my college, police, and Sheriff's work, the Highway Patrol was said not to investigate anything. With that, only Gene's time put me over the top.

Ray Price had worked as a correctional officer and a probation officer. I found Ray extremely capable of doing the job in the private sector. I even helped him get his Private Investigator license.

When I hired him, he had been convicted of Driving While Impaired. I let Ray drive a truck I had. When he got his work license, he had to have a breath-testing device on his vehicle for him to breathe in before it would start. This helped me as much as it did restrict him because the people seeing the device in his truck knew he was ok. If the police had charged him, he would have been okay with most criminals, buying stolen hogs and feed would have been much easier, and arrest would have become more possible.

Ray became the kind of top-notch help I was talking about. He had a lot of common sense and just as much educated knowledge. He had graduated from Barton College in Wilson. Ray's work as a correctional officer and with the NC probation system gave me heads-up skills most PIs don't have.

When I had a case concerning a person in prison, Ray

could read the Records of Arrests and Prosecutions (RAP) sheet and know immediately what kind of person I was dealing with and whether they had been good or bad in prison.

Sometimes, we had to get up in the middle of the night, go to a person's home, and slip a GPS on their car. That was a hard job because they could wake up anytime and find us there, which was dangerous.

Once, my nephew put a GPS on a car just outside the door to a home. I had put him out, and he went to the house to put on the GPS. I turned around on the road and headed back to pick him up. As I was heading back to him, a deer leaving a field rammed into the side of my truck. It caused my man to think that a gun was going off. He ran down the road, thinking they were shooting at him.

Another person I hired was a young Latino boy called Junior. Junior had special skills in finding stolen pigs and stolen feed. It didn't matter where we were; Junior could contact the Hispanic community to get a buy. Usually, it would result in stolen feed or pigs. On one occasion, Junior called me and told me, "I need $60 to buy some beer. " I replied. "Junior, I'm not buying your beer for you." He immediately replied, "Mr. Quinn, you don't understand. These Mexicans, they won't tell you shit if you don't get them drunk."

On one occasion, I was in Fort Walton Beach, Florida, when Junior called me. I asked him, "What was wrong?" he replied, "I'm in the hospital; I asked the wrong questions." Junior was a great employee, making $700 to $800 a week because of his efforts.

Goldsboro Milling and Prestige Corporation hired me to buy and find stolen hogs and feed. In just a few months, we had retrieved nearly 50 stolen hogs and over 10,000 lbs. of stolen feed.

We found stolen hogs in Greene, Duplin, Wayne, Lenior-Lenoir, and Sampson Counties. In one instance, we found 10,000 pounds of stolen hog feed. Many times, we would go to a Latino House to buy a hog, and there would be five hogs lying dead on a truck. Usually, they would cost $100. So, you can see that if they sold the pig, any amount would be a profit for them and not the grower.

Bob Ivey, the leader of the Goldsboro hog business, asked me how we could prove it was stolen feed from Goldsboro Milling Company. I told him we had to have a tracker that could 100% prove Goldsboro Milling Company owned this food. Both Bob Ivey and his brother, Ted, were like their dad. Harry Ivey, before them, had become someone I trusted and valued all their friendships. Bob asked what needed to be so that there would be no doubts that the food we found was Goldsboro Milling's. The lab for the milling company came up with a tracker placed on plates in Russia to identify their plates. It would show that it was their feed when used with certain chemicals. For example, when cowboys stole cattle, people stole hogs, and we were tasked to stop them.

I and the Latino youth (Junior) went to the home of a Honduran woman in Duplin County. She said that she would sell some food for our chickens. We bought two drums and returned a few weeks later to buy two more. We contacted the Duplin Sheriff, and they obtained a warrant. We found 10,000 lbs. of feed at her home. When tested, it was proven to be a Goldsboro Milling feed. Goldsboro Milling did not sell their feed, so she could not have obtained it legally.

In another instance, we bought a pig from a man in Duplin County. While my employees waited, the man left. I followed him to a hog farm in Lenoir County run by Goldsboro Milling. When he returned, he brought a dead pig in the bed of his truck and sold it to my people.

Since we knew where it came from, we just had to tattoo the pigs on that farm. Then we returned and bought another pig. I again followed, and my men got the pig for $125.00, which the mill reimbursed me for. We found the tattoo and notified the sheriff in Lenior-Lenoir County, and they charged the seller who worked on the farm.

The man who worked on the farm asked the serviceman what was happening. When he saw the tattooing, the serviceman told him we were selling this bunch to Japan and that they had to be tattooed. The man did not suspect anything until he was arrested.

In Greene County, we did the same thing: bought pig feed twice and reported the evidence to the Sheriff. Three farm employees were arrested and convicted.

On one occasion, Ray and I went to a home in Raleigh and placed a tracker on a truck on the street. A confidential informant told me the car was owned by a suspect selling stolen hogs.

That night, at about 11 p.m., using the GPS tracker, I saw the truck on a farm in Lenior County. I called a friend who was a Captain in the Duplin Sheriff's office and notified Lenior County. I then went to the scene and waited. The captain met me there, and so did a Lenior County deputy.

We entered the farm as we observed lights leaving the farm and found the truck with the tracker, the one from the car in Raleigh, coming towards us down the driveway. We stopped him at the entrance to the farm and found seven bags of corn feed in the back of the truck, along with a 30-06 rifle in the truck's cab. The feed had been stolen from that particular farm. Using the tracker, a feed test showed that it belonged to Goldsboro Milling.

One case involved buying a stolen hog. When we picked it up from the seller, it was in a blue bag with a Department of Agriculture stamp. The seller was getting it from a worker at a slaughterhouse in Warsaw, and it had already been inspected. The seller sold it to me for $100. The original salesman made much less. The Sheriff tracked it back to the Slaughterhouse in Warsaw, and my work was done. However, Goldsboro Milling gave me the pig. I cooked it and had a barbecue for my people.

The man was arrested and pleaded guilty in court. The mill received restitution, and the feed itself was saved. We bought many pigs that were stolen from other ıpanies. We notified them and gave the evidence to ;ir investigators.

In another case, a young man contacted me about his ex-wife, who was trying to get higher child support. She had moved in with another man, violating the original support agreement. Ray and I watched the home where the woman was living and saw a man leaving and entering the house. Still, there was no evidence that the couple was living together. We could not prove he stayed with her in her home without the children. One day, we saw a school bus picking up a young boy.

I called the client and asked if his son was with him, and he replied, "Yes, why?"

Getting a child on a school bus takes a lot of time, so I directed him to contact his attorney, who could obtain that information while I alone could not.

The lawyer got it, and to be sure it was true, the mother had arranged with the school to pick up and drop off the boyfriend's child. She dropped her request for higher child support when we went to court.

I investigated cases of infidelity and even prisoner release cases. Wives are cheating on husbands, and husbands are cheating on wives.

In three cases, within weeks after the divorce was final, the cheating spouses were dead from something other than the client, such as karma, I guess. Accidents, cancer, and pneumonia got them and fast.

As a licensed investigator, I made cases in more than five counties and developed hundreds of cases, from accident cases to infidelity, larceny, and prisoner release. I worked on each case with the highest level of integrity I could find. I worked in custody cases where the parents of a child had put the child in a foster home. I was able to show that the birth parents had no care for the children and were negligent of the child and out driving impaired and partying. They had an accident, and not just one parent, but both parents were together and charged by the trooper.

One case was alarming. A sister hired me to try to get her brother released from prison after 17 years in prison. He was convicted of murdering a mother and her two-year-old daughter. During a robbery, he robbed the mother. What was disturbing was that the codefendant was the teenage daughter of the murdered woman who opened the door and let him in.

In 17 years, the inmate's behavior had put him in a jail cell inside a prison and again in jail inside that jail. He was violent, according to all records, and showed no remorse at all. Based on what I found and reported to his sister, he would be a danger to society and have no chance of being released. It was terrible news, but she took it with gladness that I had found something for her.

I worked as a Private Investigator in North Carolina for ten years. Last year, my license needed renewal, and instead of attending a week-long class where I might catch COVID, I decided to retire again. I had a great time and made much money, but the money goes while the memories of each case remain. Today, I visited the local Bojangles for breakfast and did what my wife needed me to do. Life is a lot easier if your wife is happy.

I made quite a bit of money as a private investigator, but you know when it's time to stop, and I also knew.

I loved being a Police Officer in a small town, a Deputy Sheriff in a small county, and a state Trooper in North Carolina.

As I said, it's not always running your own business that you enjoy because of the stress, and it possibly was that stress that gave me a quadruple bypass in 2015. The love of my family that kept me going and my friends only added to the pleasure.

Over the years, I have met many legendary men, from Howard Mitchell to Wilberdean Shirley. Wilber was my friend, and he said it better than I did at my retirement dinner from the Highway Patrol: "There is nothing I wouldn't do for Bronnie Quinn, and I know there is nothing he wouldn't do for me."

He meant it, and he knew I did, too. We lost Wilber last year, and I miss him every day.

One person I knew was probably unimportant to many people, but he was critical to me. He drank a lot when I met him, and he was the butt of jokes for many, but Richard Moulton was a friend. He worked for me for about four years, keeping my home and flowers growing and looking sharp.

He came to me and told me he had cancer and asked if I would take him to the military graveyard in Goldsboro. I did, and he told the administrative contact there that he had been a young man in the Navy for six years. He got a grave, a casket, and a vault with a monument for his site. He told the lady at the cemetery to give the information to Mr. Quinn. He said he was going to see that he was taken care of.

Then he told my wife to see what cremation would cost. Sherry checked with a friend who worked at a nearby funeral home, and the cost for cremations would be $3000.00. Richard bought an insurance policy and left me as the beneficiary, for which I paid for his funeral.

When I went to his home to empty it after his death, there was not the first whiskey bottle in it.

He never had much, but he gave my family and me much love. Hopefully, Richard knew how much we loved him. Richard was my friend, and all he wanted was to be mine.

Richard stayed at my home with our dogs the night before my dad died. Sherry was staying with her dad as he was also in hospice care. When I got home at about 7 am, Richard told me my friend George Casey had arrived. I asked him what George wanted, and he replied, "I don't know, but he brought the fire truck." I told Richard, "He must have been looking for a donation for the fire department," Richard said, "No, he was here to put out the fire I started."

It seems Richard had set the entire side of the farm on fire.

What was so perplexing was that when the fire department personnel asked him for my phone number so they could call me and notify me of the fire, Richard told them, No. I think he has enough trouble right now" and wouldn't give them my number. Richard was found dead one morning by friends when they went to check on him at his home.

I handled his service with all the dignity and respect I could give him. I occasionally go back to the cemetery and speak to him and to be alone with my friend.

He was my friend, and I sure miss him.

As a young man in college and while in law enforcement, I made some mistakes that could have placed the label criminal on me. I won't go into them because the statute of limitations may not have passed. While I am genuinely thankful that things turned out the way they did, I regret some of my actions and some of the things I did. That is why I named this

book Trial and Error.

My earlier behavior would have made me unwanted as a friend and unneeded by my family. Only the care and protection of God and some good people who cared for me kept me free from ridicule or worse. I remember one situation in Gates County where Sergeant Herb Conway called First Sergent Jim Minton and asked, "How much time could I get for something I did?". I won't go into details, but let it be clear that it was a bonehead move. This book is to tell anyone interested in law enforcement or private investigation, whether it's working for a lawyer or a private person, some of the things you can do and many of the things you should not do.

Chapter Ten: Reflections on Life

I'm 70 years old this year, and throughout my life, I have felt that I had someone guiding me in everything I did. That dream about walking on the moon was absolute. I really cannot explain it, but it happened just that way, and so has my life.

I had two serious relationships before I met my wife, but neither was as serious about me. Soon after, I found my wife, Sherry.

When we got married, I told her, "Don't get used to me being here because I got a feeling I'll be dead and gone before I am thirty." Sherry was serious enough about our relationship that she watched over me. I took care of myself and ensured that if there was anything health-wise that I should have checked, I did. My health was of prime concern to her, and so I lived.

In addition, someone was walking with me. Maybe I'm wrong, but I have never been deeply religious. I have had my faith in a God. Unlike many, I have always believed in a supreme being with me from sunup to sundown and always in between—someone who may not be like your God but was special to me.

I really cannot explain it, but it was based on morality and love more than anything else. A divine being was always with me, like Santa Claus. He saw me when I was good and evil and knew both. More than that, he knew my heart and if I meant for things to be good. Of course, I got credits when I was good and felt the heat when I was terrible. Somehow or some way, I've made it this far.

I really can't explain it, but it has worked for me. Over the years, while in law enforcement, I asked my divine person to protect and walk with me, be there if I ever got in trouble, and help me all you could when I was too dumb or weak to help myself.

There was one more thing I asked my Lord for. If it was his will that I should die at the hands of another, Lord, please give me the power to take them with me.

I don't mean to imply that my thought process was mainly based on Christian thought or Christian Philosophy, but it worked for me. I asked God, or at least my God, that if I was to die on the road, please give me the power to take them with me. Somehow, in some way, I did not want Sherry and my boys to have to go through a trial of my killers. Somehow, I have survived.

Now, don't get me wrong. I read my Bible and believe in a God of love. Maybe that is the reason I'm still here.

Only once was my faith tested. Not when I was in patrol school, although I may have been tested without knowing. Not when I had my heart surgery, because all along, I thought he was with me. It was when I was moved from Gates County. I felt down.

Maybe my God wasn't watching me, but he was testing me. My biggest obstacle appeared to be drug dealers. One man was working at Planters Peanuts in Suffolk, Virginia, legally making under $20,000.00 a year but could afford a new car and home. He could buy his kids a new car and house and always paid cash for them. The Elizabeth City Police Department started an operation called Snowball. It dealt with drug pushers. I gave them information about this guy. When they searched his bank account, they found that he had $800,000.00 in cash hidden away. Afterward, I was the one who had to move, and the Highway Patrol said so.

I read the Bible verse about God providing for the flowers in the field and the birds of the air. When I went to church, my good friend and pastor, Bobby Hewitt, preached on that verse. Never once knowing I was having a problem, Bobby spoke and gave me the will to believe that things would be all right. I prayed and prayed, and somehow, each checker fell in place.

BRONNIE QUINN

When we moved to Wayne County, the mobile home that Daddy had given us was overturned when a wind gust hit it. We replaced the windows for $100. After it was turned over, it was fine. Mr. Gordan Best of Best Sand and Gravel turned it back over with the help of George Humphrey's Wrecker Service, setting it up. Neither of these men charged me a dime or even sent me a bill.

Still, I had a home in Gates County. I couldn't sell it. I sent money to the bank each month to pay for it and not live there. I found out the drug dealers would see people looking at my home and would stop and tell them that the house was infested with termites and that they didn't want my house. That was not True.

One day, I was at Mr. Alvin Singleton's store when a man walked in and noticed that I appeared to be worried. "Mr. Quinn," he said. "What is on your mind?" Looking at him, I told him about my home in Gates County and its comforts. My family struggled in a trailer, and I was forced to send my paycheck to a bank there, so I couldn't do better.

"Mr. Quinn," he said. "Leave ¼ of what you're paying that bank on the Neuse River bridge tonight, and you won't have that problem tomorrow."

I couldn't do that. Two weeks passed. Again, I saw another man at Mr. Alvin's store who asked me the same thing. Again, I replied to his answer. Then he said, "The man told you what to do, and you won't listen." I still couldn't do that.

After five years, I sold that house. We made a little money on it. However, I know that without Sherry, I would never have gotten rid of it. She worked out the sale with her excellent negotiation skills when it collapsed. It was Sherry who made it with less at times when we needed more.

Maybe it was a test or just meant for me to suffer. Today, my faith is strong, and my life is still good. Two of the drug dealers are dead, and the one with $800,000.00 lost his money to the lawyers.

I don't want to sound too sanctimonious, but God brought

Sherry into my life. It was my God who protected me. He also provided for me, like the birds of the air and the flowers of the field. It was my God who walked with me. His footprints were in the sand when I struggled because he was carrying me.

My God gave me friends like Howard Mitchell, Abraham Saunders, Wilberdean Shirley, Gasper Gonzales, Deloris Kennedy, Curtis Waters, Jim Winters, Matt Brinkley, and even Larry Jones. My God led me through the valley of the shadow of death and brought me this far.

I have done some boneheaded things, but God has brought me this far, and I think I'll stay with him.

This book was titled Trial and Errors for a Purpose. My life has been a series of trials and errors. While most folks' lives are sometimes like that, mine seems to have been an actual series. Like most people, raising children, working, and even having enough money to survive, at times, was a challenge. Don't get me wrong; I made good money. There were challenges, particularly with raising kids. No one ever had a book telling them how to raise their kids right.

Sherry was brilliant because she kept them in sports and off the streets. Of course, Travis always wanted money to spend on shoes and clothes, while Bret never told you what he wanted, so we never really knew. We tried to keep up with both, but sometimes they weren't with us. You never really know what your kids will do when they are away from you. You pray that it all works out.

Somehow, they both got things right. Both have gotten profitable jobs and are doing the type of work they want. Bret is a vice president for a local bank and monitors their computers, and Travis recruits Locum Tenon doctors in the medical field. I am so very proud of them both.

I'm smart enough to know that my days are numbered, even with Sherry watching over me like a hawk. I'm just two years younger from the age when my grandad died. I'm ten years away from the age when my dad died. While I hope I'm lucky. I expect it any day, as I have for the last 40 years. It's all been a series of trials and errors. Along the way, my faith has increased. I hope I have done something right along the way to help me enter that place, which is not made by hands but eternal in the heavens.

Bronnie Lee Quinn-

I was born in Kinston in 1953. I grew up in Jones County in a small community named Comfort—the eldest of two children. My education was in public schools. I graduated from Jones Senior High School in 1972. During high school, I worked in a grocery store. After high school, I attended East Carolina University and graduated with a Bachelor of Science in Criminal Justice in 1982. My job history has dealt with law enforcement in all aspects, from investigations, fraud, loss prevention, traffic, accident investigations, and writing tickets for city, county, and state for over 30 years. After my government jobs, I worked for a law firm for six years as a private investigator. In 2010, I opened Quinn Investigations, LLC. I decided to retire when our country was going through the COVID-19 pandemic in 2020, and I needed the training to maintain my license. Through the years, I've told stories about my experiences with people telling me I needed to write them down. I am now writing them down so my family and friends will have them to show how life was while I was here.